# Wealth Mindset Secrets: Discover How To Get Rich, Make Money Online & Boost Your Wealth, Income, Prosperity, Confidence & Success With 2 Books In 1 - Make Money Blogging & Entrepreneur Millionaire Mind

Timothy Flynn & Jeffy Cooks

# Table Of Contents

# The Make Money Blogging Blueprint:

How To Begin Making Money Blogging For Profit Step By Step - Earn Passive Income With An Online Business (Includes Writing, SEO & Affiliate Marketing Secrets).

By Timothy Flynn

book are for clarifying purposes only and are the owned by the owners themselves, not affiliated with this document.

# Introduction.

Did you know that over 1 billion people use Google?

We live in the information age.

And as consumers, we're constantly scouring the web looking for answers to our questions, tutorials and tips.

But as the saying goes, money follows eyeballs.

And if you can create a blog that drives traffic from Google, social media or anywhere else on the web, you can make money.

The beauty of this is that all this takes is a bit of persistence and hard work.

Why? Because...

- You don't need any money to get started
- Anyone can rank their website on Google if their blog is good enough
- Plus you can create a blog that you're passionate about

In this book, you're going to learn how to create your own profitable blog, how to market your website and the secrets behind monetising your blog - so that you can generate a passive income stream from it.

So if you're ready to start making money blogging, let's dive in and get to it.

# Chapter 1. The Basics Of Blogging

Blogging is an industry that's taken the modern online world of entrepreneurship by storm.

Virtually everyone interested in online business uses blogging as a platform to promote whatever it is they have to offer – whether it be an ebook, handmade products or simply entertainment/information.

This book will give you a fully comprehensive guide to setting up your first blog and how to make money blogging…

What Is A Blog?

The definition of a blog is often misconstrued as being a space to which individuals post daily content related to their personal lives and hobbies. Many people avoid blogging for this reason, as they feel they simply have nothing exciting to offer and couldn't generate enough interest to earn money.

**Thankfully, a blog can focus on anything you wish.**

The term 'blog' simply just means a page that is regularly updated. Blogging in itself has no limits and could be based on your own interests, popular interests, news, health – you name it. Your decisions lie total in your own hands.

Blogging can, with a large enough following, be turned into a full-time job. When you're learning how to make money blogging, try and soak up enough information as possible. Every piece of information you get could be incredibly valuable in the future.

For example, utilising ads will generate automatic revenue that simply requires you to keep the blog running and watching money flow into your account. Advertisement will be covered in depth later in this article.

So buckle up – we're off on a whistle-stop tour on how to make money blogging!

# Chapter 2: Finding A Niche

Okay, so the very first thing you'll need to do before even thinking about blogging is deciding on your niche. A niche is simply a fancy word for a specific segment of the market that your blog will focus on.

Deciding on what to focus your blog on can, for many, be one of the most challenging parts of the process. In a world of fascinating subjects (as well as millions of pre-existing blogs) it can be very difficult to decide on the topic of your blog.

Although no area is wholly unique, you as an individual are. Your own spin on the content you produce will set your blog apart from everybody else's so don't worry if your niche feels to generic or 'mainstream'.

How To Choose A Niche

So how do you go about choosing a suitable niche?

First and foremost, you need to have an interest in the area you choose. As a blogger, you'll be posting regular content (daily at first) to your site focused solely on your niche. If you choose an area that doesn't interest you, you simply won't have any motivation to write.

Although choosing a niche that you wouldn't mind writing about every day is important, it would also be unwise to go with a topic based purely on your interests. While you may find particle physics thrilling to research, if there isn't a gap in the marketplace (an area which isn't currently being explored much but is attracting a lot of interest) for this topic then your blog simply won't succeed. The key to your success is attention. If you blog doesn't draw people in, it will not be profitable.

Tips For Choosing A Great Niche

As discussed before, your niche must be attracting some attention if it is to be at all successful. But how can you possibly know which areas are doing well or not? Asking around won't exactly give you much to go on and questionnaires are expensive to distribute – so how?

Two words. Keyword research.

Keyword Research

Keyword research is absolutely the driving force behind the success of any site. Without it, businesses would be taking stabs in the dark and simply guessing what people are interested in.

Keyword research should be conducted before naming your blog as well as the titles for posts you include. Be sure to get a feel for the wants and needs of your chosen market before committing to a domain name.

Have you ever wondered why sites such as Google and Bing are completely free?

Well, technically, they're not. You are in fact exchanging something in return - your information.

Popular sites such as Google's AdWords as well as Keyword Keg both have sections that allow you to search using keywords to get an idea of how often people are searching for words online. If you want to create a fishing blog, for instance, searching words related to fishing will tell you how much attention those words are attracting online.

Google keeps track of what its visitors are searching for online every month and sells this information to companies (although the bits we'll be using are all free). Through their system called 'Google AdWords', Google offers a free keyword research tool that allows you to gain an insight into how often different words are being searched for each month.

You can find this keyword tool via:

www.adwords.google.com/KeywordPlanner

To get started, simply open up the keyword planner and punch in a word you'd like to research. Have a play around to begin with, exploring any ideas you've already had for your site and any that come to mind. Try as many words as you can think of that surround your subject.

Let's use a website about wood for example. You could type in oak, furniture, wood, reclaimed vintage etc - just have a play around and make notes on what you find.

The sweet spot here is to find a product that attracts over 4,000 monthly searches. This value is large enough for you to make money but small enough that you avoid fierce competition. A product with, say, 400,000 monthly searched will be rife with competition as this huge amount likely means that this niche is already being harvested.

Some pointers when conducting keyword research:

- **First and foremost, don't be afraid to use keyword research tools other than Google AdWords.** Yes, Google may be the number one search engine but it isn't the only one and competition is fierce so don't neglect the wealth of research tools available. Here are some of the best keyword tools I and many others use (don't stick to just one - try to use them all together). Ubersuggest, Keyword Keg, Bing Ads (which works the same way as AdWords but for Bing and not Google) and Keyword Shitter - yes, I'm serious. Try a number of these tools together to gauge the activity of the internet as whole and not just of Google alone.
- **Don't neglect long-tail keywords.** These are keyword phrases that exceed just one word - 'reclaimed oak furniture' rather than just 'oak', for example. The trouble with using single keywords is that they're incredibly difficult to rank in search engines for. Just think - how many results are likely to be returned if you search for oak in a search engine? Thousands, if not millions. Wikipedia probably has a page about oak, some Amazon ad as well as a tonne of other companies associated with oak. Trying to rank for singular keywords is so difficult as there are so many sites out there already doing so. Long-tail keywords are much more specific and give you a higher chance of ranking highly in search engines. Take your niche and search around using a variety of different long-tail words

to get a better understanding of the activities of your demographic online.

- **Don't focus entirely on monthly searches.** Yes, keyword research is stressed as being of utmost importance in the world of online marketing, however there are several other factors to take into account. Keywords labelled as low competition with high monthly searches may be so because they offer no value and are difficult to monetise - that niche may simply be dead and unpopular. Conduct research outside of just keyword searches to get a holistic idea of how your niche fairs online.

# Chapter 3: Naming Your Website

Choosing A Domain Name.

Domain? What on earth is a domain?

Your domain name is simply the name of your website. Examples of domain names include:

- BBC.co.uk
- Minecraft.net
- Navy.mil

When choosing a domain name you'll have to choose which suffix you'd like, whether that be .com, .co.uk, .biz, .info, .net – it's up you.

Choosing an appropriate domain name that is both representative and original is key to your blog's success. Picking a catchy, snappy title that'll stick in people's minds will likely be much more successful than a title littered with numbers and obsolete characters. What I mean here is that fishingdaily.com would be a much better choice than, say, f1sh1ngd41lyeveryday.com. The first one simply looks more professional and is easier to remember than the second.

Some pointers for choosing a good domain name:

- Use as little wording as possible for convenience and effectiveness – something that stands out and is easy to remember.
- Try to be original. Understandably great site titles are hard to come by and even harder to think of, however choosing something snappy and quirky will sound better to viewers and they'll be more likely to spread the word. Making up your own words can work too so long as they're relevant to your site's topic.
- Choose an appropriate suffix. If you're running a news blog, .info may be appropriate, .com might be better for a more entertainment-focused blog and .co.uk for a blog aimed at UK citizens. .com is likely your safest and best option in most cases, though, and is far easier to remember.

Where To Buy Your Domain Name:


So you've thought of a title – now what?


There are a wealth of domain-hosting sites out there and therefore plenty to choose from. Some may offer different services to others for varying prices so be sure to search around for the best deal you can get for your site. Here's a list of some of the most reputable and well-used domain hosting sites.


- BlueHost
- GoDaddy
- HostGator

Just as a side note – sticking with a fairly cheap hosting site is absolutely fine if this is your first blog. You can always upgrade your plan if you find it lacks what you need later down the line when you have a larger following of say, over 20,000 monthly visitors.

# Chapter 4: Blogging Platforms

Your Blogging Platform.

Your domain is up and running. You've chosen an appropriate title that attracts a decent amount of attention and you're all ready to get going with your blog. Where do you start?

Without a blogging platform, you simply can't run a blog. Not unless you're a HTML wizard and know the web like the back of your hand – though you most likely aren't.

WordPress offers an easy to use blogging software that takes care of all the tricky coding for you. If using Bluehost, simply log into your domain hosting account and locate the 'install wordpress' icon. Then, choose 'do it yourself' and 'check domain' before accepting their terms and conditions.

Once you've done that, your site will be up and running – bland and empty, but it exists now and is a clean slate for you to paint however you wish.

Designing Your Wordpress Blog.

In the realm of blogging, designs are known as 'themes'. Themes can be downloaded online and are highly customisable to suit your ideas.

To choose your theme, head on over to [your domain name]/wp-admin. and log into your account.

Don't panic. Yes, there are lots of buttons and side headings on the WordPress dashboard however don't let these scare you – it's not as complicated as it looks.

Head on over to the 'appearance' side heading on the left and select 'themes'. At the top of the screen, click on 'add new' to add a new theme.

You can browse through WordPress's free themes until you find one you like or you can use their filtering feature to whittle down those that are more suited to you.

Once you've found one you like, go ahead and hit install and activate and you're good to go!

Customising Your Blog.

Your WordPress theme is the foundation for your design, however your theme can also be customised a tonne to create a site you're happy with.

First, hit 'customise' in the themes tab of your site's dashboard. You'll then be able to edit your site's design freely, changing its colour schemes, fonts, and imagery to suit your requirements.

I'd advise spending a good few hours tweaking your design to see what works and looks best. Don't be afraid to get a second opinion too, adjusting your layout to adapt to constructive criticisms.

# Chapter 5: SEO

Optimising For Search Engines.

Search engine optimisation (SEO) is a huge industry that generates billions of pounds yearly.

SEO is the process of fine-tuning your website to maximise its discoverability on search engines. High levels of SEO will ensure that your site ranks highly in search engines as opposed to featuring on, say, the 60th page of Google.

Because SEO is the key factor to your sites monetary success, we'll be covering this whole section on it.

A useful little Wordpress plugin called 'Yoast SEO' will help to increase your search engine effectiveness – just search for it in the plugin side heading of your site.

Once installed, access the plugin's settings through the 'SEO sidebar' you'll now see. Then, go to 'your info' and input your site name and details.

Then, head to 'webmaster tools' and click on the Google Search Console link. Once signed in, copy the long alphanumeric code on the HTML Tag section after 'content="' under the 'alternate methods' heading.

Next, paste this code into the Google Search Console bar back on the webmaster tools screen. Click verify once done.

Keyword Analysis.

As was lightly touched upon earlier, keyword research is absolutely key to your site's success as it'll ensure that people find your site effectively.

To begin with, make a list of different topics that you'd like your site to rank for. These may include, in the case of a fishing blog: sea-fishing, carp fishing, fishing for beginners etc.

Use this list of topics to decide on some keywords that will best describe your blog. Stick these words into a keyword researching tool (Google Adwords, Keyword Keg – whatever you choose) to get an idea of how many search results these keywords generate. This will give you an idea not only of how popular your keywords are, but also how much competition blogs focused on these words hold.

Create a bank of keywords that would be best for your blog – words that aren't marked as being highly competitive but that have a substantial amount of monthly views are best (around

1,000-20,000). Use these words as often as you can – in your titles, writing, descriptions, wherever possible to maximise the traffic your site gets.

Boosting Your Google Rankings.
Search Engine Optimisation (SEO) is hands down the best way to increase your income. The more visitors your site brings in, the higher your overall profits will be. The reason for this is that, if people aren't able to find your site, they simply won't be able to click on your links and make purchases. Therefore it is vital that you maximise SEO to increase your income.

Perhaps the best way to boost your site's ranking in the Google search results is by building **backlinks**.

A backlinks is simply a link from another person's site to yours. In Google's eyes, the more links a site has to it the more reputable it likely is, and therefore the higher it should rank in a search engine.

Therefore, your main aim when increasing the traffic your site attracts is building up lots of backlinks.

It's important to exercise some caution when building backlinks. If you go ahead and build hundred within your first month of setting up a site, Google will likely flag your site and it won't be as successful in ranking in search engines.

Aim to build a handful of links per week and gradually build up your backlink network over a longer period of time.

You should also aim to adjust your **anchor text** as much as you can. Anchor text is the line of text that will link somebody to your site.

For example, <u>Number One Search Engine!</u> is the anchor text here and is linking people to Google's site. Poor examples of anchor texts are things like 'click here' or 'visit this website' – aim to be unique in your links but also relevant to the product you're advertising.

Other Considerations For SEO.

Here's some more key tips in ranking highly on Google and maximising your monthly site visits:

- Use a domain name with appropriate keywords. Your domain name should not only be kept short and snappy as well as easy to remember but they should include some keywords relevant to your niche. Don't choose an irrelevant site title just because it sounds cool or resonates with you – if you're in this for the profit then you need to stick to the rulebook and choose an appropriate title.
- Supply decent, top-quality content. It's no good promoting the hell out of a site that offers nothing of value. Though people may end up visiting your site, they'll soon be turned away by poor content that clearly wasn't created with care. If you struggle with writing and simply *can't* create good content, you can always hire somebody else to write for you for a fairly low price. This is also great for people wishing to turn marketing into an entirely passive source of income as you won't even be required to create content, moreover sit back and watch your site tick away by itself.
- Building on this point, being sure to get regular content published is also key to SEO. If your site doesn't offer frequent, new content to be read then people will become bored and won't revisit. If you do wish to create an affiliate site centred on a specific Amazon niche that you can leave to tick away then this point isn't too much of a concern as, with low competition, the site will still bring in visitors regardless. If

you're running one site with more effort than the others, though, and wish to focus on that as a primary source of income then you should seek to publish regular content to that platform.

- Focus on building good quality links that are grounded in evidence. Link-building sites that claim to offer great services for free generally offer fairly poor quality services and won't do you much good at all. Dodgy backlinks will also be flagged by search engines and could hinder your SEO progress so try always to build up strong, credible ones.

# Chapter 6: Content

# What Should You Write About?

Now that your blogs all up and running, it's time to start actually posting some content. But what on earth should you write about?

I'll run you through a step-by-step process on how you can generate a wealth of topics for your blog in very little time.

- **What might your readers be passionate about or excited by?** If you're running a fishing blog, ask yourself what exactly might excited readers and fuel their desires. Let your ideas flow – fill your page with whatever comes to mind. No idea is a bad idea during the planning stage, it's simply more fuel for your blogging fire and will give you a great place to start in future.
- **What problems/challenges might your readers have?** Ask yourself what your audience may struggle with in relation to your topic. This may be based on your own experiences or those of others. Try to come up with a list of troubles your readers may have – with the fishing example, this may be difficulties with tying knots in fishing line, how to prepare for a fishing trip or how to avoid detection when fishing. If your blog is intended for musicians, perhaps you could explore how to overcome difficulties with finding a band, how to break writer's block or how to write original music. Whatever your

23

topic, add to your list of ideas by exploring associated problems.

- **What sort of people will be reading your blog?** What are some personality traits of your readers? Perhaps avid fisherman will be relatively care-free and emotionally stable, whilst a musician may be more charismatic and extroverted. Use these qualities to get a feel for the types of people you'll be writing for and the sorts of things that they may be interested in.
- **What might annoy your readers?** With relation to your niche, think about things that might get on your reader's' nerves. With fishing, readers may hate the noise passers-by make that scares any potential catches away. These would make great, relatable ideas for blog posts that will entice readers and perhaps open doors for some humourous content too.
- **What do your readers love?** Conversely, writing about things that your readers love to talk about/do is a sure way to increase your monthly visitors. This information can easily be gathered by looking at topic-related forums on the web as well as simply asking questions in hobbyist Facebook groups.

This list can then be used to generate a wealth of blog-post ideas. Perhaps your post tries to solve your readers problems. Maybe it captures their passions and gives them something relatable and exciting to read all about.

# Chapter 7: Your First Blog Post

## Writing Your First Blog Post.

Now that you've got a bank of ideas to write about it's time to go ahead and click the 'write' button on your blogging homepage.

Using keyword research as mentioned before, choose a title that attracts a decent amount of regular attention to make the most of the web traffic drawn to your niche.

Sentence structure is everything when it comes to writing an enticing, captivating post that really grasps your readers' attention and gives them a reason to stick around. Try to vary your sentence types to create a more natural, speech-like fluidity to your writing. Examine the following paragraphs:

*'Carp fishing is the best way to catch regular fish because carp are the most abundant species, often being found in shallower lakes that are more easily accessible to average fishers. If you're fishing to catch often then carp fishing is the way to go as it's fast-paced, will give you a lot of catches and is easy to get started with.'*

This paragraph feels clunky. It lacks dynamics and simply makes statements rather than attempting to engage with the reader. All of its sentences are factual and too long to digest easily. Now consider this paragraph:

'If you're an adrenaline-junkie like I am and love regular catches, I have two words for you. Carp fishing. Focusing on catching carp will keep you on your toes, providing you with quick and easy catches. The best part? Carp fishing is dead easy. Anybody can do it!'

This paragraph has a lot more texture and variation than the first. The words it uses are exciting and different facts are separated into separate sentences.

You want to try and follow the second style of writing when making blog posts. Avoid overly long, hard-to-read sentences that are likely to make readers hit the back button and find somewhere else to get their information.

**Below are some useful pointers to ensure your sentences are engaging and easy to read:**

- Don't make sentences longer than they need to be. Make your point, make it exciting and move on.

- Separate large chunks of texts into separate paragraphs to ensure that readers aren't faced with massive, ugly blocks of text. They'll simply just skip ahead.
- Use adjectives and verbs where appropriate to make your writing stand out and more exciting to read.

How To Stay Motivated.

Granted, at first you'll be motivated enough to probably smash through 4 or 5 posts over your first few days of blogging. Although it may not seem so, there will come times where you simply don't have the drive or time to blog every day.

Unfortunately, life gets in the way.

Picture this. If you have a doctor's appointment or a meeting with friend, you'll likely stick to it. You'll feel motivated to actually go ahead with your plans because you've pre-arranged them. This is exactly how we'll be staying motivated to keep blogging.

Before you even start posting you'll want to create a blogging calendar. This is simply a list of dates that you'll be writing for your site.

Firstly, take a look at a calendar and decide which days of the next week you'll be posting.

In the first week of your blog's existence, your main goal is simply getting content out there. Aim to have written 10 posts within your first 16 days of blogging – 20 in your first month if you can. If people stumble across your blog, like what they see but find that it lacks content and isn't giving them more of what they'd like then they simply won't return and you'll have lost a potential subscriber.

Decide which days of the week you'll be writing, what you'd like to write about and who will be writing (this'll likely to be you to start with).

Open up a spreadsheet (Microsoft Excel, Google Sheets, Apple's Numbers – whatever you prefer, it doesn't matter) and put this information in.

Add your dates along the left side (perhaps you choose every 3 days to post like I have (right)). This is also a good opportunity to decide on your keywords so you can avoid conducting time-consuming research when you come to write your post and just get on with it.

If you can, try to schedule around 20-25 blog posts. That'll give you 6 months worth of content planned and ready to write when you've chosen to.

Scheduling Blog Posts.

Additionally, if you find you have more time and motivation than you'd planned for, WordPress allows you to schedule blog posts.

This means that, once you've written your post, you can decide when it'll go live. If you've written an extra post in the morning, for example, but have committed to posting every three days, you can plan for this post to go public in three days time.

I'd strongly recommend scheduling posts when you find the time to do more work than you'd initially planned to. Not only will this free up your time but it'll also reduce your stress levels as you'll spend less energy thinking about what you have left to do and more about what you're doing right now/have already accomplished.

Getting Feedback From Your Audience.

Now that you've scheduled your posts and have the groundwork complete for getting content out there, you're ready to start receiving feedback from your site's visitors.

There are many ways to do this and the simplest is probably adding social media buttons to your page. These can be super simply implemented by using WordPress's menu features. All you need to do is sign into your social media accounts (depending on which platforms you are signed up for) and the buttons will pop up wherever you wish.

Additionally, you can add comment sections to your site. These sections give readers the opportunity to add their opinion beneath your posts. You can also decide whether you allow comments to appear freely or with your control. That way, you can disallow any negative comments that you feel are unhelpful and hateful.

Contact us pages can also be created with WordPress. These display contact forms into which visitors can input their contact details and send you personal emails. These emails can be a great way to connect with visitors and build up your blogging network.

Constructive comments you receive can be used, if you wish, to improve your site and to maximise your traffic by providing your audience with what they want to read.

It is important, though, that you don't let these comments define your blog. If you receive negative, hateful comments you cannot let these get to you and influence your decisions. There are bound to be people out there that don't like what you do. This isn't your fault and it also isn't something you can change, so don't worry about it.

# Chapter 8: Social Media

# Promoting Your Blog Through Social Media.

Social media is an absolutely booming industry, populated by millions of not *billions* of people worldwide. It is for exactly this reason that social media is a goldmine when it comes to directing people to your blog.

I would highly recommend to anybody building up a large following for many reasons. Having a large following simply gives you a wider influence and reach in any field. It gives you the ability to send messages to a huge audience that wouldn't typically be reachable in a day-to-day setting. It can also be an excellent platform to promote yours or somebody else's business/service. For you, it'll be an invaluable way of directing followers to your blog and increase your audience.

I personally use Crowdfire as a way of building up followers. Crowdfire allows you to connect your social media accounts and generate a following by 'copying' other people's followers.

Crowdfire will look at your social media page and allow you to put in your blog's main areas of interest (be it beauty, travel, fitness etc.). It'll then give you a list of daily prescriptions – simple tasks that'll boost your followers very quickly.

These prescriptions include small things such as sharing a number of recommended posts based on your followers' interests, following 50 daily followers of popular pages in your field and liking your followers posts. You can also choose to unfollow your non-followers if you wish and 'whitelist' certain accounts to ensure that you don't accidentally unfollow them. Additionally, you can post through Crowdfire's app and choose to publicise your post at the 'best time' as decided by Crowdfire's technology based on peak social media times.

I would highly recommend Crowdfire as a free service perfect for beginner accounts. If you wish to upgrade your plan from free to a selection of 3 paid services ranging in features then you can do so when you deem it necessary, however the original free plan is more than enough for the beginner blogger.

# Choosing Your Content

Using apps like Crowdfire alone, however, is not enough to build up a strong and interested following.

If you simply use the features of the app/others like it and don't take the time to publish decent, regular content then your followers will either be inactive, dummy accounts or genuine accounts that get bored and soon unfollow your account.

The key to any success is consistency. It is vital to post regularly, multiple times a day even if you can, to ensure your followers remain engaged and interested in your account.

Although tempting, **do not** clog up your social media feed with promotion. Have you ever unfollowed an account because of its annoying and constant pleas for followers to go and buy and buy some product/like a page?

I certainly have – you don't want to be *that account.*

Although you should aim to promote your blog regularly (once a week perhaps), try to do this discreetly. Don't outwardly beg people to check out your site. Try instead dropping links to your blog posts where they're relevant to your audience's interests. On another blog of mine, for example, I posted about the most romantic places to travel to the week before Valentine's Day. This post wasn't labelled as my own and thus it came across as a friendly pointer rather than a desperate advertisement.

Keep up to date with current affairs and be sure to post regularly to captivate your audience and keep their interest.

# Chapter 9: Monetising

## Monetising Your Blog.

If you wish to turn your blogging hobby into a full-time career then you will eventually need to monetise your site. This simply means adding to it features that will generate income. Below are listed some of the best ways to do this.

Selling Products.

So are you wondering how to make money blogging by selling products?

Through your site you can create 'shop' pages that give information on products that you wish to sell. If you're already a manufacturer that makes products, this can be an excellent platform to begin selling them online to a related and interested audience.

Alternatively, if you do not already make products, there are tonnes of ways to get started. These products could simply be design templates or even eBooks that can be sold through your online store. The great thing about digital products is that they can be sold an infinite number of times as they are multiple copies of the same thing.

Dropshipping is even possible with your blog. Dropshipping is simply the process of selling products that you do not actually own. When a customer makes a purchase on one of your listed products you simply have it shipped directly from a supplier to their house. That way, you never have to store the product nor do you have to package and ship it.

Advertising.

Still wondering how to make money blogging?

As well as selling products, there is also a tonne of money to be made through advertising the products of other people.

This is advertising…and it's one of the top ways to earn when beginners are figuring out how to make money blogging.

The first and most popular way of advertising other people's' products is using a tool called AdSense run by Google. The system works by allowing you to put your advertising space (just a small section of your site – a rectangular square advertising a product) up for sale on their site. Different companies will then bid for your ad space, their bidding values depending on your blog's reach. Whoever bids highest will then take your advertising spot. Each time a visitor of your website clicks on an ad you will receive a small profit that'll vary between companies. Although your payment per click will likely be very small, if you generate a large audience and have thousands of weekly clickers then you can generate a lot of money through AdSense.

The best part about AdSense is that it's totally free. All you need to get started is a Google account and a website. Companies will also be paying *you* for advertising their business.

It would be unwise, however, to create an AdSense campaign if you have a very small following. For the effort you'll put in, the amount you'll be paid by companies will be very little. If your site doesn't attract much attention then you won't make enough sales to make your ads profitable and they'll simply go to waste.

AdSense is, nevertheless, an excellent way to earn money on your blog when you have a large enough following to make it profitable.

# Chapter 10: Affiliate Marketing.

Next up on the list of how to make money through blogging is a system known as affiliate marketing.

What is Affiliate Marketing?

Affiliate marketing sounds a lot more complicated than it actually is.

Affiliate marketing is simply another form of paid business advertisement.

Many thousands of companies offer what is known as an 'affiliate program'. Individuals/businesses that sign up to be a part of this program will be sent links (as in website links - clickable URLs or images) that direct people to a specific product purchase page. These links can then be placed on a website/other online medium to be viewed by the rest of the internet.

So why is this any use in online entrepreneurship?

Every single time a person clicks your link and makes a purchase on the advertised product, you'll be paid a percentage directly by the respective company. Set up enough affiliate links on a high-traffic website and you'll have yourself an entirely passive method of making money online.

Almost all big-name companies out there have affiliate programs available that anybody with a website can sign up for. Once you sign up to an affiliate program, you'll be sent a number of links (as in website links) that will take anybody who clicks them to a product purchase page. The sort of links you see everywhere from an online hardware store to YouTube that advertise products to the general public.

Here's where the money comes in. Every time somebody clicks on these links, as before, you'll be paid directly to your bank account. Depending on the type of program you're a part of, companies will pay you either per click or a percentage of each sale made.

Let's say you ran a travel blog and signed up for Thomas Cook's affiliate program. In a blog post all about travelling to Thailand, you dropped a couple of affiliate links for some of Thomas Cook's holidays to the country, priced at £1,500 per person per holiday. Cook's scheme offers affiliate marketers, let's say (hypothetically speaking), 20% per sale made. Your blog attracts, in this scenario, 2,000 monthly visitors and a measly 1% of those visitors make a purchase on the Thailand holiday.

1% of 2,000 is 20. 20 people make a purchase on the holiday which totals at £30,000. You'd make 20% of this, which equals £1,500.

So, in that scenario, you'd earn £1,500 profit on a single affiliate link by selling to just 1% of an audience of just 2,000 monthly visitors. These numbers are all incredibly small (2,000 isn't a lot a visitor's, £1,500 isn't the most expensive sale and 1% is very small) and so, in a real life situation wherein you're running a highly successful blog you'd likely make at least 10 times this amount.

And affiliate marketing isn't at all limited to travel alone! There are thousands of ways to utilise affiliate marketing available out there and there's guaranteed to be on fitted to your blog.

The great thing about advertising is that money will be earned almost entirely passively. Although, yes, you'll need to maintain your blog in order to keep your audience and have people actually follow your advertising links, the money you make from these advertisements are totally passive – they won't require you to really do anything in order to earn money.

# Chapter 11: Clickbank

Clickbank.com is perhaps the most common platform through which affiliate marketers to set up their online empires. It offers millions of affiliate links and attracts a tonne of reputable companies, perhaps holding the top spot in the world of affiliate program databases, but how what is it and how can it be used effectively?

What Is Clickbank?

Clickbank is a website that offers over 30,000 different products to affiliate marketers. As a Clickbank member, you'll be able to choose the most relevant products and drop links to those products on your website.

Products available on Clickbank average at around $40 each and offer about 50% in commission rates (working out at $20 per product purchased). Products that sell better may offer commissions as high as 70/75%.

**Learning how to make money with Clickbank is incredibly easy - and this chapter will teach you everything you need to know!**
Choosing A Product.

Now that you've chosen a niche you'll need to decide on the types of products you'll be selling. This is where Clickbank comes into play.

First and foremost, you'll need to <u>create a clickbank account</u> - this is completely free and easy to do.

One step of signing up will involve choosing an 'ID'. This is the name that will show up in your affiliate links and ensure money is paid to you so make this appropriate - something simple like passive50 or kingpassive10.

Once you've made an account you'll be all ready to go.

How to choose a Clickbank product

So long as you've conducted your keyword research to deem which products are attracting the right amount of attention, all you need to do is choose products in this field that are listed on Clickbank.

If you want to learn how to make money with Clickbank, check out these pointers for choosing your Clickbank products:

- **Is the product worth your time and effort?** Take a look at the product's commission rates and its price. You should try to avoid products that offer you lower than 50% commission, as these simply won't be worthwhile when there are other options that'll earn you so much more.
- **Is the product actually being purchased?** Clickbank lists its products in order of popularity by default based on the number of sales affiliates have made within the last 8 weeks. Don't discount products towards the lower end of the scale. Although these may be less popular at the moment, they could still increase in demand and prove to be a valuable option with little competition.
- **Does the sales copy of the product meet a high standard?** Click on the product and take a look at the description if offers, the 'sales copy'. If this is no good then people are unlikely to proceed with buying the product, thus wasting your time. Try to stick with products that provide decent sales copy to avoid missing out on sales.
- **Does the product's seller offer support for affiliates?** Decent businesses will offer more than just affiliate links,

such as extra promotional material, mailing lists with regular batches of useful information and readily available support with your marketing. Avoid vendors that only offer affiliate links - you should be getting much more than just this.

Getting The Ball Rolling

You've found your products to market and you've set up the skeleton of your website ready to customise to suit your affiliate business. What next?

Now you need to add some value to your site and give people a reason to actually visit your site and make a purchase rather than read and click away.

The best way to do this is by offering top quality information about the products you'll be marketing. We'll be doing this by writing articles about each of the products you choose - articles no more than around 400 words in length that sum up why readers should go ahead and make that purchase.

Thankfully, much of the information you'll be needing to write about your products will already be given to you in the product's sales copy - the text added to its purchase page that tells customers exactly what the product is and what it does.

When writing your products, always consider the following three pointers to ensure your content is of a high quality:

**Who:** Who is going to be receiving your article? With the example of oak reclaimed furniture, perhaps your audience will be mainly young couples interested in old-style, rustic furniture for their new homes. You should therefore consider this type of buyer's background and their interests and tailor your writing to impress this demographic. The article will mainly be reviewing the product with a link to follow. Ideally, your article will answer any questions your audience may have and leave them with nothing more to do other than go ahead and buy the product.

**What:** What is the product? Here you should give a fully detailed description of what the product is and how it can be used. Summarise the information already given to you in an informative and exciting way. Be positive in your writing and speak of the good qualities of the product as much as possible.

**Why:** Why should your site's visitors purchase this product rather than other, similar products from different retailers? Maybe this particular products is easier to use than other products. Maybe it's incredibly simple to assemble and will add a unique, rustic touch to your home. Give your reader no reason not to go ahead and buy the product - be as convincing as you can and leave them feeling as though they *have* to buy this product and no other.

After you've written the first article, keep writing others for the rest of your products. You may wish to set them to go public at a later date, choosing to publicise a number of articles over a one-month period, one every few days days. This way, you'll constantly be sending out new unique content without you having to keep writing articles to post.

Facebook & Product Funnelling.

Product funneling is how you can utilise Facebook and your website to maximise your Clickbank sales.

It involves sending people from a Facebook ad to a 'presale' page, and finally to that all-important 'buy product' page.

1. **Facebook Ads:** When you're first learning how to make money with Clickbank, Facebook ads are an incredibly effective way to direct people to your website and

persuade them to buy the product you're marketing. Facebook ads are super simple to setup, simply head on over to their ad creating section and create an advert for the product you'll be marketing. Be sure to include a representative image as well as a snappy, appropriate title. From here, you'll be linking people to your pre-sale page - the part of your website includes all of that persuasive and high-quality information about the product itself.

2.  **The Pre-sell Page:** Your ad should link people directly to this product description page, hence why it's vital that the information you offer is of a very high standard and is effective in persuading people to make a purchase. This page is what takes people from that Facebook-browsing social mindset to more of a buyer's mindset. You should explain exactly how the product you're marketing is able to solve the very problems you identified that they may have earlier in this guide. Then, go ahead and solve that problem with your product link.

3.  **Product Link:** Finally, once you've got them warmed up, redirect them to the product you're marketing. So long as you've given them top-quality information about exactly why they should buy this product, your viewers should be left with no questions to ask and ready to go ahead and click that all-important 'buy' button, landing you a decent sum of commissions.

# Chapter 12: Amazon

Amazon, being perhaps the top dog in all global online retailing, is an excellent option for the newbie affiliate.

Amazon offer an affiliate program that allows you to advertise virtually any of the products they offer. The scheme is called 'Amazon Associates' and it's super easy to sign up to. Once you do, you can pick and choose the links that best suit your site. Amazon offers up to 10% in advertising fees and these will be paid directly your bank account.

Here's some advantages of being an Amazon affiliate:

- Amazon offers tens of thousands of products, all of which you can become an affiliate for.
- There are **always** new products to promote.
- Amazon is an established, reputable platform and so people are much more keen to make purchases with the as opposed to other, less-renowned sites.
- Amazon's niches are all fairly uncompetitive.
- With Amazon's excellent sales recommendations, people typically end up spending far more than they initially intended to. All sales made through your link will earn you commissions.
- You don't need to manufacture or sell your own products – you'll be earning money simply by providing a link to somebody else's.

Just as a side note – yes, you would earn significantly more money if you were to sell your own products online. However, being an affiliate rather than a direct salesperson requires **far** less maintenance and can run in the background whilst you get on doing other things.

An Amazon affiliate site can even be created and left entirely to run on its own, requiring you to do absolutely nothing to maintain it in the future. This is because Amazon's niches are very low competition and so you won't be battling with other affiliates all of the time to try and get the most sales & not be overrun by their content.

Getting Started With Amazon

In order to setup a profitable Amazon affiliate platform, you should always promote products in a 90/10 way.

What I mean by this is that 90% of your products should be high-end, £100 or more. These are the products that'll be generating most of your income as they'll be paying more commission.

The other 10% should be lower-end. These are the products that you'll be hoping to sell frequently – the more products you sell, the higher your overall commissions will be. If you sell upwards of, say, 20 products week as opposed to 5 then your commission percentage per item will be higher due to your ability to sell more frequently. Essentially you become a more valuable affiliate marketer and thus are paid more highly.

The following criteria should be followed when looking for high-end products to sell:

- Products should be £100 or more.
- They should have at least 10 product reviews (to ensure that the product is popular and still being sold).
- They should have a rating of at least three stars – promoting inadequate products will only complicate the process.

- The product should also have at least four or five other, similar products that you can promote. This way you'll have a number of products to market rather than just one.

However, there are some affiliate products to avoid on Amazon including:

- TVs
- Cameras
- High-end watches
- Laptops/computers
- Phones

## Why?

…Simply because *everybody* chooses these niches when starting out and they've become incredibly oversaturated. If you're trying to make money out of a niche that everybody's already milked for all its worth you'll simply be undermined by competition and struggle to attract any customers.

It's always best to explore more obscure, less-mainstream niches. Rather than selling something generic like luxury watches, instead explore the fashion industry by delving into more specific areas such as men's boots or blazers. These products still offer a lot of value and thus high returns on commission, however they're less commonly exploited and thus have much more profit available.

# Chapter 13: Flipping Your Website:

You've probably heard of flipping before although often it's described using a wealth of other names – if you caught our retail arbitrage article you'll have learned a little about flipping and how to do it there. Flipping, in essence, is the process of buying low and selling high.

The stock market, a far more prevalent industry, follows this principle on a much larger scale, allowing investors to buy and sell to make full-time income. By 'flipping' a product, you're turning it around and boosting its price to earn you a profit for doing very little work.

So What is Website Flipping?

Flipping in itself is a simple concept to understand, however you may be wondering how exactly this principle can be applied to websites?

Buying and selling businesses and stock is a far riskier process than purchasing websites. Not only are prices significantly lower but your work input is too.

As mentioned in previous articles, whether a blog, news site or ecommerce store, setting up a website of your own is an excellent opportunity to start earning a passive income. The only downside with starting your own site from scratch, though, is that you'll need to build up your audience over time to make any significant profits.

Without traffic, your website will simply be a goldmine never discovered. When you buy a website, however, anybody that searches for that specific URL will be redirected to the new website you decide to create.

To put this into context, let's use a hypothetical example of BBC News. Imagine BBC decided to abandon its news website, advertising it on a domain-selling site for a high price. If you chose to buy this domain name, anybody that searches for BBC News will instead find your site. Thus, all of BBC's web traffic will become your traffic.

Many pre-existing websites are, to put it bluntly, very poorly run. There are a plethora of popular sites out there that attract a large number of web-users but simply don't draw in any money. Why? Because those that run the website have not maximised the potential of advertising. It's incredibly simply to drop a handful of advertisements across a blog page, for example, using a company like AdSense. In doing this, anybody that clicks on these ads will generate you a profit. You, as a website flipper, can buy these websites and monetise them to draw in profits, maximising their potential as advertising platforms.

To put a timeline onto this jumble of steps, here's exactly how you'd go about flipping a website:

1. First you'd purchase a site after having decided on which is best for your goals. More on choosing an appropriate site in the next article.

2. Next you'd improve the site, tweaking any design faults and implementing money-making tools such as ads and affiliate links to send money your way.
3. Then you wait and promote your site. Allow profits to come in and use them to make adjustments to your site – consider your target audience and tailor your ads to them.
4. And when you're ready and feel as though your site has made enough money you can sell it on, making back your initial investment with a nice amount of profit too.

Advantages Of Flipping Websites
- The biggest advantages of buying a pre-existing site is that you will not need to establish an audience yourself to make a profit. You'll be buying a site that already has had time spent growing its audience thus removing the need for you to do so.
- Buying a site to earn money allows you to make your own schedule, working when is best for you.
- You'll be able to sell the site once you're finished with it, further boosting your profits. In flipping websites you'll be purchasing them, improving them, using them to make money and then moving on to the next site when its resources become depleted.
- You can use website flipping to make money without any of the hassle of a typical day job – no interviews, bosses, geographical ties – you are your own boss.
- Buying a website is far easier than creating one yourself, especially if you lack computer skills and would struggle to do so alone.

Disadvantages Of Flipping Websites

- Flipping websites has the potential to use up a lot of your time which could prove to be an issue when also juggling family life, other jobs and social events.
- You may end up overpaying for websites as it's incredibly difficult to gauge exactly how much sites should cost.
- Supply could well meet demand making it tricky to sell your website on. You are very much at the hands of the market here, however your investment fees will thankfully be significantly low and thus you're not likely to lose out on a lot of money if things do fail.
- The starting costs could, however, be high depending on the quality of the site. Although your investment costs will be significantly low if you so wish, the cheaper the site you purchase the more work you'll likely have to put into improving it.

Buying a Site

Alternatively, if you want to hit the ground running, you could buy a pre-existing website to flip. This strategy will avoid you having to create a website from scratch and could give you access to a wide audience instantly without having to build up a following. If you buy a website that's been around for a while, its owner will likely have already put the hours into SEO and attracting attention so you won't need to do this yourself.

Before buying a site, though, it's crucial to do your research to know exactly what you're buying. You could end up spending hundreds on a site that appears to be a goldmine but instead generates no money and leaves you with an empty pocket. Some sites simply just aren't meant for making money.

Before buying you'll need to find out:

- Why the site is being sold.
- Why it is/isn't profitable.
- Why the site isn't being monetised (if it isn't).

How to Buy A Site To Flip

- Look for a site that has a large community. Purchasing a website that has forums and a sociable audience is a great place to begin. It is likely that a web-owner with a hobbyist audience is not looking to monetise their site but instead provide a platform for like-mindeds to communicate and share information. This is a great opportunity for you to buy that site and utilise this enthusiastic audience to generate a profit. Try to choose a community that will give you a decent selection of affiliate products to market.
- Buying competing sites. Additionally you could purchase a website competing in the same niche as you. Sites of this sort will already have established their audiences and generated a decent following within that field. That way, you won't need to reshape the site to suit your chosen niche and can build off of a pre-made site.
- Search for sites that use popular keywords. Choosing a site that operates in a niche with very popular keywords is another good place to begin. If you can find a low-priced site that operates within a niche that is soon to become very popular, buying it now and selling it on later when said sites are higher in demand could earn you a nice amount of profit for doing very little.

- Buying a site purely to sell it. Buying a website that is failing simply because its owner has poor advertising skills and isn't skilled in SEO can also provide a nice cash turnover for you. Choosing a website that is operating within a nice that's just about to take off is a great place to begin. Buying a site that's been poorly run, improving it to maximise potential within its popular niche and selling it on will earn you very nice chunk of money. Be sure to sell the site before the marketplace catches up and that niche becomes saturated to maximise your profits.
- Purchasing based on what you currently sell. If you already run a site/blog of your own you can direct your web traffic to your new site so long as it shares the same niche. This way you'll be able to build generate a lot of traffic instantly that actually care about your site. Generating traffic is often the most difficult and time consuming aspect of setting up a successful website and so bypassing this step by using existing websites is a great way to save time and maximise profits.

How To Buy A Website.

We've covered *how* to purchase your website and what exactly website flipping entails.

The next topic we'll be tackling is how to buy a website that will make you more money?

There are thousands, millions even, of websites out there, a tonne of which are up for sale. Choosing the best and most profitable one may at first seem like a daunting task. How do you know which sites have the best potential? Which websites should you avoid? How do you decide which niche to explore?

In this article, we'll teach you exactly how to buy a website & flip it for more money.

Choosing Your Niche

One of the vital components to running a successful website is publishing consistent content. You're going to need to post a lot about your site's niche to draw people in and engage your audience. Therefore it's best to choose a niche that you're passionate about, or at least have a significant amount of interest in.

Perhaps you're particularly in fishing – choosing a website with a hobbyist audience interested in fishing would be a great place to begin as you'll actually enjoy writing content and won't become tired of it. Choosing a site focussed on magic ticks, however, may bore you to death and leave you unmotivated to continue with your site, wasting the fees to paid for it and the time you've spend improving it.

Additionally, choose a niche that is alive and isn't on the verge of becoming extinct. Choose something that is popular right now – use Google AdWords to get an idea of what niches are trending/have a large audience. If you choose a niche that isn't attracting a large audience then you simply won't earn money through your site.

When you deploy ad campaigns onto your site you'll be paid depending on how many clicks they get. Visitors of a particular niche are more likely to click links related to their hobbies and so it's vital to gauge the interests of you audience to maximise profits.

How To Buy A Website: Deciding Your Budget
A website can be sold for anywhere from £40 to £40 million so deciding on how much you should spend can be a tough decision for somebody just starting out. Really, the choose is entirely yours depending on how much money you're willing to put in.

Buying a cheap site may at first seem like a great way to minimise risks and maximise your initial profits. However, low-end websites typically aren't fully optimised for search engines and won't have much potential to earn you money. If a site is up for sale then you'll need to find out why.

If its owner has decided that the most profitable thing for them to do is flog it as it simply isn't making money then perhaps the site won't work out for you either. In some cases, though, inexperienced web-hosts will sell a site in hope of earning a decent sum of money when actually they're abandoning a gold mind and selling it off for far less than it would be worth in the long run.

Most importantly, if you're a newbie you'll have very little experience and thus won't know much about the costs of websites. Many website flippers overpay for sites in the beginning, spending far too much on a site that doesn't hold much potential at all. To gauge how much a website should cost, check out Flippa's 'just sold' section to see the prices being paid for different types of website. Use this alongside tools like Google AdWords to get a feel for the market and an idea of the sort of prices you should be paying for a site.

As a general rule of thumb, aim to spend no more than half of your budget on a site. Avoid forking out almost all of your funds on a single site, leaving you with next to nothing to fall back on. Make a small investment and get your website-flipping feet wet before diving straight in at the deep end.

Competition

You need to check out the competition for your site's niche before making a purchase too. Using sites such as SimilarWeb can allow you to find out important information about any competitors such as their page views per month, time spent on the site and bounce rates.

Carrying out a keyword search using a platform such as Google's Keyword Planner can also allow you to gauge the attention your niche is receiving, as well as the attention your competitors' are attracting.

Don't be fooled, though. Although choosing a niche that has many millions of visitors may seem like a fantastic opportunity to start earning megabucks from ad-clicks, a huge traffic base probably hasn't gone unnoticed. It is likely that a very popular niche is being exploited by many other entrepreneurs and so it's vital to choose an area that has just the right amount of visitors.

Choosing a niche with around 100,000 – 150,000 search results on Google would be a good place to begin. A site with this volume of traffic will be generating enough attention to earn you money without sitting on a market filled with competition, making it easier for you to take the top spots without having to compete.

How To Buy A Website: A Few Things to Keep in Mind
- Explore multiple search platforms such as Facebook and Bing, not just Google. There are a wealth of sites out there that generate a tonne of daily visitors so don't neglect them.
- Add value to your site with great content. If the website doesn't include a blog already, insert one and post top-quality content. This will not only draw in new readers but give them a reason to stay and revisit your site in future.
- Don't sell your site at the wrong time. Once your growth rate slows down to around 30% a year it may be wise to sell it on, however cutting your profits short in the hope of getting paid a few thousand for your site while it still has **plenty** of room for growth is not a wise idea. Picture the site as a mine – you want to gather all of its resources before moving onto the next mine in search of more. Don't be greedy and lose your common sense.

How to Improve Your Website's Value.

So you've bought a site and feel you've maximised its potential. Now you're looking to sell it and make the most out of the work you've put in. How exactly? This post will explain exactly how you can maximise your profit when selling a site.

1. Purchasing a premium domain name.
A site that has a premium domain name is worth considerably more on a less sought-after domain name. For example, 'www.fishing.com' would be far more valuable than, say, 'www.000fish1ng021.com'. Having a premium domain name gives the site much more value as it has the potential to land a tonne more visitors. Obscure names like the one mentioned before are simply never going to be discovered and look tacky & unprofessional.

Paying to upgrade your domain name to something more concise and representative is a great way to add value with very little work. Aiming for simple titles that don't have a lot of unnecessary letters/numbers is a good place to start. Try to ensure that your name suits the website and isn't totally unrelated too.

2. Build an audience on social media
Developing a large following through social media is a great way to add value to your site. Even if your site has great advertising schemes in place (affiliate marketing, AdSense, ecommerce etc.) it may be worthless without any traffic. You could have every advert in the world with the potential to make

thousands, however without visitors you simply won't receive a penny.

You could do this through Twitter, Facebook, Instagram or Pinterest. Apps such as Crowdfire are invaluable tools that'll help you build up a strong following interested in your niche with little effort. The app allows you to search for keywords or popular pages and follow anybody following these areas with the simple tap of a finger. Then, once the people you've followed decide to follow you back you can just as easily tap unfollow, giving you a strong follower:following ratio.

Any followers you build up through social media can be directed straight to your site. Social media is an area to explore simply because it attracts a *tonne* of visitors every single day. Having a strong follower base will instantly add value to your site as it gives it far more potential to make money.

3. Advertisement

A huge amount of value can be added to a site by implementing advertising schemes.

Affiliate marketing, in a nutshell, is a scheme that most companies have in place whereby they give links to clients to place on their website. Each time a person clicks that link and makes a purchase, the client will be paid by the company for advertisement. It's dead simple to sign up to affiliate programs and Amazon has a huge section dedicated to it, allowing you to add a tonne of links to your site for an array of different products. Using these links across your site will add an awful lot of value as it simply gives it much more potential to earn a buyer money.

Many affiliate programs also offer discount codes – codes that you can publish to your site and offer to customers allowing them to buy products at a discounted price. When customers purchase a product using your code, you'll receive a cut of the payment. It's really that simple.

There are a number of strategies that work best when it comes to selling affiliate products:

- Focus your site on selling one product. This usually works best if you're selling a popular product and are offering top-quality information for it.
- Selling multiple products can also be effective and doesn't require much differentiation in design.
- Starting a blog website that focuses its products around a specific niche related to its audience can also be a great strategy when using affiliate links to make money.

4. Increasing your prices

Building onto point number 3, if you already have advertisements in place then you may wish to raise the prices you're being paid for these. If your site is generating a large amount of traffic then you should be able to speak with your vendor and get a raise on your commissions.

Alternatively if you're site generates money through ecommerce – actually selling products from your site – you could try raising the products' prices to gauge the maximum profit available on those products. Test raising your gradually and see how this affects your sales. Once your sales begin to reduce, you've reached the maximum value that your product can be sold for without affecting sales.

5. Diversification

Diversifying the site's revenue streams can be another excellent way of adding value. If you're relying solely on an affiliate program to generate money, expanding the sites streams of income will make it more attractive to a buyer as it'll have many areas to fall back on.

Consider selling products directly from your site rather than selling for others. You may choose to add a 'store' section to your site from which you can sell products. These could be dropshipped (products sold but kept in stock elsewhere – all you'll need to do is have them shipped to customers) products, products created by you or simply products that you store and ship yourself.

Alternatively, if your site is already focused on selling products then consider adding an AdSense campaign or some affiliate links. These are super easy ways of adding value to the website and generating more income without having to handle any more products. If your shop already attracts a large amount of customers then those customers are highly likely to follow links that are specific to their interests.

And there you have it – a whistlestop tour through the world of website flipping and how to maximise the value of your site. As always, the key is persistence. However you decide to ramp up your site's value, stay consistent with your methods and don't lose track of your site's metrics. Keep an eye on its monthly visitors and how doing different things affects your monthly visits to keep doing the right thing.

Chapter 14: How to Sell Your Website.

It's all well and good knowing what website flipping is, how to improve a site, how to increase its value etcetera etcetera, but the key purpose to flipping is to sell your website once it's finished with.

At its heart, the underlying principle of website flipping is buying a site, improving it and selling it for an increased value. Therefore it is vital to know the best strategies when it comes to how to sell your website.

It's deceptively easy to sell your website for far less than its worth because somebody offered you a seemingly high price for it. While a £1,000 transaction for an immaterial, digital display may seem like a blessing, knowing exactly how much your site is worth and how to sell it effectively is key to making a profit. This article will cover exactly that.

How Much is Your Website Worth?
To put it simply, your website will be worth however much somebody is prepared to pay for it. There is no universal tool to calculate the exact value of any site – it simply depends upon the potential an individual buyer sees in it.

Now, I know, this isn't particularly useful when people are asking how much you're going to sell your website for and you have no idea how to value it. It's key that you don't underestimate your site's worth and sell it off for much less than it's actually worth – especially after putting a load of work into it.

A good place to start is to aim to sell your site for around three times to six times its yearly earnings, without the inclusion of taxes. Say your site rakes in £5,000 a year – aim to sell it for a minimum of £15,000 – the amount you'd earn in three years of running the site.

Where Should You Sell Your Site?

**Flippa**.com is perhaps the most well-known and reputable platform for selling websites. It has more websites than any other platform available for sale and attracts the largest number of buyers – over 850,000 people are currently registered to purchase sites. Flippa is incredible easy to use and provides the option to upgrade listings to attract more attention. Being the top-dog of the website marketplace, Flippa is a well trusted platform that brings in serious buyers willing to buy high prices for websites.

**BuySellWebsite**.com is a great site to use to find either well-established or just-started-up websites, differing in prices depending on the establishment of the site. BuySellWebsite also offers the feature of creating a two-month-long listing with a free extra month that'll feature on the site's homepage.

**InternetCompanyForSale**,com charge no commission on sales made from their sites, giving you 100% of the price paid for your site. You will, however, need to pay listing fees for the site again depending on the level of establishment. Well-established sites cost just less than $60.00 to sell and start-up websites cost just under $40.00.

## Audience

As with any form of sale, taking your demographic into account is key to using effective sales techniques appropriate to a specific audience. Advertising a site as being an excellent tool for blogging and creating a community will render useless when trying to sell to a bunch of online entrepreneurs hoping to earn stacks of cash from your site. Tailoring your selling tactics to your audience is vital to attracting a high volume of buyers looking to pay decent prices.

## Research

Rather than going completely with your instincts, search around for other sites that have made a decent amount of money in sales and use their advertising techniques. What sales tactics work best? How are they interacting with their audience to maximise their profits? There's nothing wrong with pinching a few ideas here and there so long as you're not completely ripping off somebody else's ad campaign.

## Searching for Buyers

An alternative to creating a listing for your site on platforms such as Flippa is to search out buyers directly. This way, you'll avoid any listing fees/commission payments and can take 100% of your buyer's payment.

As for where to find buyers, Ebay is an excellent site to use to advertise. The only issue with Ebay is that it's entirely auction based and relies on an automated bidding system. Negotiation and haggling are great ways to bump up your price to get the most out of your site. Ebay is by all means a good place to start, however your listings will have to be very good in order to get paid full price for your site. If you wish to avoid automated systems and have the ability to haggle, forums may be a better option.

A forum such as SitePoint's SiteSell area can be used to list your site and increase the amount of people it reaches. You can browse around the site to see how much other sites are selling for to gauge how much yours is worth. Once a buyer discovers your listing and is interested, they'll contact you asking about your prices and make you offers. This way, you'll be able to see wht buyers are willing to pay before deciding for them how much your site is worth. As we said before, your site really is worth just as much as people are willing to pay for it.

You want to avoid cutting yourself short by underestimating your site's worth and accepting a seemingly reasonable payment when actually you could be earning far more. If you can, let buyers offer you a price before you give them one. Don't be afraid to haggle, either. If you feel they're offering a lower price than you could ask for, try raising it slightly to see how much they're willing to pay.

## THE END

And there you have it!

A fully comprehensive, start-to-finish guide on how to create your first successful blog and how to make money blogging.

# Unlock Your Millionaire Mindset:

Discover How To Make Money Online With
The Millionaire Mindset!

By Jeffy Cooks

This document is geared towards providing exact and reliable information in regards to the topic and issue covered. The publication is sold with the idea that the publisher is not required to render accounting, officially permitted, or otherwise, qualified services. If advice is necessary, legal or professional, a practiced individual in the profession should be ordered.

From a Declaration of Principles which was accepted and approved equally by a Committee of the American Bar Association and a Committee of Publishers and Associations.

The information provided herein is stated to be truthful and consistent, in that any liability, in terms of inattention or otherwise, by any usage or abuse of any policies, processes, or directions contained within is the solitary and utter responsibility of the recipient reader. Under no circumstances will any legal responsibility or blame be held against the publisher for any reparation, damages, or monetary loss due to the information herein, either directly or indirectly.

The information herein is offered for informational purposes solely, and is universal as so. The presentation of the information is without contract or any type of guarantee assurance.

The trademarks that are used are without any consent, and the publication of the trademark is without permission or backing by the trademark owner. All trademarks and brands within this book are for clarifying purposes only and are the owned by the owners themselves, not affiliated with this document.

# Chapter 1. Why Anyone Can Make Money Online & How You Can Get Started:

As you're most likely already aware as you've came across this article – there are a plethora of ways to earn money online out there.

...So can you make money online – the answer is yes!!

So why doesn't everybody just quit their day jobs and take to the internet?

Well, unfortunately for many of us, self-doubt has taken over the decision-making computers that are our brains and decided for us that we simply 'can't do this' and 'can't do that', hindering our ability to ever even try.

Can You Make Money Online? Of Course! Here's A Few Examples:

Blogs, YouTube videos, affiliate marketing, retail arbitrage – these are just 4 of thousands of money-making opportunities out there that just about anybody can do. Yes, that includes **you**.

Regardless of whether or not you're a skilled wordsmith, an adept in web design or a master of Photoshop, working from home, thanks to the invaluable advancements of modern technology, has never been easier. Seriously, working from home is easier now than it ever has been in the past which is exactly why you should not doubt your skills to do so.

Many jobs that can be completed online require a little common sense and basic computer skills – nothing more. Being able to string together nicely-structured, fairly intelligent-sounding sentences, having decent conversational skills and, above all, the motivation to succeed can get you incredibly far in the online world.

So long as you have a computer, internet connection and the capacity to work independently, free from other workers you most certainly have the ability to work online.

But How Can You Make Money Online? Here's How To Get Started:

There are an absolute tonne of ways to earn money online out there – literally thousands. But how should you go about choosing the right and most profitable ones that work for you?

Well, to begin with, let's look at a three of the most popular and flexible ways.

- Affiliate marketing. Affiliate marketing is an incredibly powerful and flexible tool when it comes to establishing a steady, automated flow of income through the internet. Thousands and thousands of companies out there (Amazon, Nike, Adidas – you name it!) have affiliate programs available for anybody to sign up to. Once you sign up, the respective company will send you some links to products that are relevant to your niche. Then, you simply drop these links across your page, whether it be a social media account, blog, website or YouTube channel and get paid commission every single time a person clicks on it! The great thing about affiliate marketing is it has no strict requirements and so you can run an affiliate business through any platform you choose.

- Upwork.com Many freelance workers use the popular job-finding site Upwork. Upwork allows employers to post job opportunities to their pages that can be searched for depending on the needs of each worker. You may advertise yourself as a graphic designer, a content writer or a web-creator. Once you're setup, you can apply for whichever jobs suit you best and, if you succeed in your application, be paid to work online. I personally have taken on many positions through Upwork and have been working in coffee shops and sofas on my laptop for around a year now.

- Photography. Don't scroll down. In today's world the idea that you need to be an expert cameraman with top-of-the-range equipment to succeed in the photography is entirely false. Thanks to the building of sites such as Shuttershock, virtually anybody can earn money through photography. Even if you don't have the best camera in the world, simply taking photos that are likely to be highly demanded by companies looking to add images to their site will earn you decent money. Shuttershock requires users to pay membership fees monthly which they then use to pay individuals/businesses that provide the images. You'll be paid every single time a person downloads your image. The beauty of photography is that it can be done almost entirely passively. Once your photos are up, you'll receive payments for as long as they continue to be downloaded.

I have purposely picked out what I consider to be the most widely accessible and skill-less ways to earn money online, however there are many, many more.

The beauty of these three techniques are that none require any expert knowledge or qualifications yet can generate enough income to allow you to work entirely from home.

All are also incredibly flexible and can be tweaked to suit an individual's personal expertise. Affiliate marketing can be done through social media, websites, blogs and many more online platforms. Blogging can even also come in the form of 'vlogging'/video blogging – so even if you lack writing skills then you can deliver information in the form of video.

Upwork offers endless job opportunities that are updated with new posts virtually by the minute so there's bound to be a position there that's just right for you. Photography can also cover a wide range of areas. Photos can be taken of literally anything you have access to and, if you'd prefer to work entirely through the web, software like Photoshop can be used to create digital imagery to sell on/templates.

**So, reverting back to the original question, can you make money online?**

…Absolutely!

So Can You Make Money Online Easily?

The internet is the most diverse, interconnected, opportunistic resource around that can be harvested by just about anybody with access to it.

If total geographical freedom and cutting loose the chains that hold you to your current 9-5 job sounds right for you then don't wait any longer.

So now that you don't need to ask can you make money online – because the answer is obviously YES! Now just find what suits you, do your research and pursue the career path you've always wanted.

# Chapter 2. How To Overcome & Build Your Persistence.

"I Can't Make Money" Is A Fear That Everyone Has Faced At One Time Or Another.

I'd tried making money online for years before I made any decent money.

I went through every single emotion...

I tried.

I failed.

I f**ked up completely.

I got bored.

I was distracted.

'I can't make money online' was a fear I faced almost everyday.

And eventually I gave up on a TON of my online business ventures.

But the biggest problem is just that...giving up. And giving up way too early...

You Have To Conquer Your Fear.

If you give up too soon, you won't reap the rewards of your hard work.

The concept of making money online is beautiful.

BUT…

The reality is an insane amount of hard work.

And when most people realise just how much hard work it takes, they give up far too early.

Especially when starting a business comes with no guarantees.

And that's exactly why most people can't make money online.

It's a hard, frustrating game that demands an incredible amount of patience.


**The Dream VS The Reality.**

One of the reasons why people think they can't make money is that the dream is extremely different from the reality.

Being an entrepreneur is an incredible concept. BUT it takes a hell of a lot of hard work upfront…

For example:

All those digital nomads you see on Instagram, posting pics of their office on the beach. (yea that happens)

In reality, they work like dogs.

They're seriously motivated. They spend everyday focusing on that dream. And they're incredibly hard working.

Most digital nomads I've met are earning less than $1,000 a month…

…Some of them had been working for years & still earning pennies.

And that's really not unusual.

I don't pity them. I don't mock them. I don't doubt that one day they'll be crushing it.

Because success doesn't happen overnight.

It takes years & years of hard work.

Sure, there are exceptions – but in the majority of cases, it takes a long time to earn decent money.

And unfortunately, most people don't have that kind of determination.

They would't be able to handle the stress of the job.

And in end, they get so frustrated they give up.

If you can't make money online yet, and you're not willing to make sacrifices, you may never be happy as an internet marketer.

Because to become successful at working online, you need to be prepared to deal with some seriously testing situations.

Picture these moments for example:

- Not knowing how much money you're going to make all year.

- Not even knowing whether you'll make a dollar at all.

- Seeing your best friends earning at least 2X, 3X or 10X the amount of money you do.

- Facing the fear that you 'can't make money online' whilst dedicating every minute of every day to your online business.

- Dealing with some really crappy customers 24/7.

- Never taking a day off. (Seriously, I can't remember the last time I took a day off.)

- No pension or retirement fund until you start making decent money online.

…And that's just a few of the problems you'll face on a weekly basis.

Worried You Can't Make Money Online? Shiny Object Syndrome Is Your Biggest Enemy…

Most people can't make money online because they don't have the determination:

They don't want to spend 5 years of their life working towards something that pays very little reward in the meantime.

…And this whole vicious cycle leads to shiny object syndrome.

Here's how Shiny Object Syndrome is plaguing the internet marketing world:

1. You worry you can't make money online with your current idea.
2. So you look at other internet marketers who boast of the 'easiest, fastest & most hassle-free' way to make money online.
3. You jump onto a new idea & abandon the old business that you invested months of time, hard work & money into.
4. Then you realise that the new idea isn't perfect either – so the vicious cycle starts all over again!

Distraction is a HUGE issue – and it's incredibly seductive.

Because whether we realise it or not, we're always looking for an excuse to explain why we can't do something.

That way if we fail, we can blame it on something else.

It relieves your fear.

So if you find yourself looking for the next shiny object that will 'make you a million dollars in 24 hours', STOP!

Because it's total F**KING BS!

And instead, keep grinding on your current project.

Making Money Online Is All About Your Mindset.

Making money online is all about how you motivated, determined & focused you are.

It's basically your whole mindset.

And if you haven't got the right mindset, you can't make money online.

Because your poor mindset will lead you into a trap:

- You'll bounce one from idea to the other, without sticking to your guns.
- You'll blame your failures on someone else.
- You'll be stuck in a vicious cycle of shiny object syndrome.
- You'll lack the motivation you need to succeed in this game.

Just remember this:

You've got an abundance of time. You can't rush success. You just have to see it through & keep going.

Work hard. Grind. Hustle…And stop trying to get everything overnight!

Thousands Of Internet Marketers Believe Life Is Always Greener On The Other Side…But There's No Golden Ticket.

How To Stop Feeling Like You Can't Make More Money.

If you want to get good at something, you have to persevere.

It's the same if you're playing football, learning chess or becoming a doctor.

You're building a skill set, one that takes years to master.

And no one else can do it for you.

No coach.

No guru.

No fancy course that's giving you unrealistic expectations.

Sure, you might make money in the short-term but internet marketing is a long term game.

And you have your whole life to make money online.

Now there are some exceptions:

I have a few friends who made six figures within their first year. And that's awesome! But if it doesn't work out for you, don't lose hope!

In fact, the people I've met who made six figures online are still working like dogs.

They have so much drive & love for what they do that they're working even harder now to reach a million dollars online.

But that's the sort of mindset that will make you successful!

Just remember that you have an abundance of time.

There's no rush – especially if you're enjoying the journey.

And with so much time on your hands, you can afford to work at a steady pace whilst staying focused.

So change your mindset. Be prepared to persevere. And stay 100% focused.

That's all it takes.

# Chapter 3. Why You Should Never Give Up.

Does this sound familiar?

..You've read every money making book.

…Watched every course about becoming a digital nomad.

…And wasted a ton of money along the way.

In fact, some days you feel like going back to a full time job and giving up your dreams of travelling the world whilst working online.

Nothing seems to be working:

Your sales are slow. You have no customers online. Even if your social media following is lame!

But before you give up on making money online, please understand this:

This game is all about persistence.

Give up on making money online now and you'll waste all the hard work you've done without reaping the rewards.

I would HATE it if you gave up now. That would be a disaster!

And that's why I've written this article…

So here's 10 reasons why you should never give up on making money online…

1. You Can't Fail If You Don't Give Up.

What would you do if you were absolutely certain you would succeed?

Whether you want to make a decent side income or hustle online full time, it's impossible to fail if you don't give up.

The best things in life take time. All you need to do is invest it wisely.

But you have an abundance of time. And that's all that making money online will cost you.

Everything you need to make money online can be bought with your own time.

- You don't need to hire anyone else.
- You don't need to spend big on paid advertising.
- You don't need to pay for a fancy course or the latest book by a business guru.

And believe me, if working online was easy, everyone would be doing it!

To create a successful business online, all you need is time and hard work.

You can <u>make money online without spending a single cent – as you'll</u> <u>find out here</u>!

That's the formula for making money online – don't be fooled by anything else!

You literally have the rest of your life ahead of you.

So what have you got to lose?

## 2. Every Successful Person Has Faced The Same Problems As You Right Now.

You've got to respect the process when it comes to achieving anything.

You're on a journey right now. And it's the same journey every successful person has travelled.

There will be loads of times when you want to give up.

In fact, I can almost guarantee this:

Every single online entrepreneur has thought 'should I give up on making money online?'

It's 100% natural. It's the journey to success.

And no one can take that journey for you – it's you and you alone.

Need proof?

Let's take a look at a few successful people who could've given up on BUT didn't:

- JK Rowling was <u>rejected dozens of times, received Government Aid and couldn't even afford a computer</u> when she wrote the Harry Potter series.
- The Beatles, who sold over 250 million records, were told they had <u>"no future in show business"</u>!
- Albert Einstein couldn't speak until he was 4 years old. In his school report, his <u>teachers claimed he'd never amount to anything</u>.
- Walt Disney <u>was fired for "not being creative enough"</u> – he still holds the record for the most Oscars won by one person. On one of his earlier ventures he even went bankrupt.

…All of these people were told they weren't good enough.

…All of them could've easily quit.

…Yet all of them went on to be incredibly successful because they never gave up!

Failure is just one small step on the road to success. Don't let it fool you.

3. You'll Have Wasted Hours, Days, Months Or Even Years Of Hard Work.

You've done the hard work.

…Not it's time to reap the rewards.

Give up on making money now and you'll lose the hours, days and months of hard work you've put into working online.

There are tons of digital nomads I've met who were literally a stone's throw from making money online – yet they faaailed at the last hurdle.

They simply gave up, packed their bags and decided to head home.

So here's a few examples of where you could give up but need keep going:

- Dropshipping websites with no customers.
- Fiverr accounts that aren't generating enough sales (YET!).
- UpWork profiles with bad reviews.

…So many people experience the above and decide to give up on making money online.

But here's the thing:

These are all just challenges along the way. You don't need to give up!

Persist and you'll reap the rewards.

It just takes time.

## 4. You'll Build Habits For Success.

If you can learn how to launch your own business and never give up on making money online, you can apply that same experience to become successful in almost anything in your life!

Making money online. Gym. Hobbies. Sports. Losing weight. Competing.

These are all examples of where persistence counts.

…And the list is endless.

So don't give up on making money online – because you're about to learn a skill that literally pays off for the rest of your life!

## 5. You Knew This Was Going To Be Tough.
Let's be 100% honest…

You knew that starting an online business was going to be seriously hard work.

And don't even try to tell me you believed all the get rich quick schemes!

If you've already made the choice to try and make money online, you knew just just how difficult it was going to be.

…You know that it requires endless hours of hard work, hustle and grinding.

In fact, that's what I love about this lifestyle!

You get to see the results of all of your hard work:

The sales, the customers, the website traffic grow exponentially as you continue to keep going.

Now let's contrast this to your other main lifestyle option…

Say you're working in a full time job for a corporate company.

No matter how hard you work…

No matter how many weekends you waste…

No matter how many hours you spend in meetings…

You can still end up facing a whole bunch of shitty situations that are out of your control.

Redundancy. Pay cuts. Ruthless colleagues.

These are all out of your control!

But if you work online for yourself, you can have almost complete control.

You'll benefit from all the hard work you put in.

You'll have complete job security as long you never give up on making money online – and that's the beauty of it!

Why give up control of your life to someone else?

6. Success Comes From Failure.

Failure is incredibly character building.

It makes you stronger. It makes you adapt. It makes you become more resilient.

And if you give up on making money now, you won't become stronger. You won't adapt. You won't become more resilient.

…You'll simply learn to quit when things get tough – and that will never help you!

All the traits to become successful grow from failure. You have to keep going or you won't grow as a person.

There's just one thing you need to do:

Learn from the mistakes you make.

Think of business like a game:

The more you practice, the better you'll get.

You have to hone your entrepreneurial skills and keep them sharpened.

And if you quit whilst everyone else persists, you'll lose the game by default.

You'll voluntarily give up everything you've worked for.

And you won't get the chance to grow as an entrepreneur.

So why give up on making money online now?

7. Your Future Self Will Thank You.
...Seriously!

All the hard work you put in now is worth it.

Just imagine reminiscing in 5 years time and thinking back to the point that you decided not to give up on making money online...

That will be an amazing feeling!

...You'll look back and remember all the times you kept going.

..All the times you could've quit but didn't.

…All the times you thought about quitting but you didn't listen, you just kept going.

It's kind of like the <u>marshmallow theory</u>:

You can eat 1 marshmallow now or you can receive 2 marshmallows later.

In other words, make a small sacrifice of hard work now and you'll reap the benefits later.

This is all about self control. And it pays off, BIG time!

The truth is, if you <u>master your mindset</u>, you'll master your future success.

8. You Have To Go Beyond Your Comfort Zone To Grow As A Person.

Feeling frustrated?

Wanna give up on making money online all the freakin' time?

Well, that just shows you're leaving your comfort zone!

You gotta crack a few eggs to make an omelette right?

And that feeling of frustration you're getting is simply your mind and body growing as you become stronger.

It's like the gym:

You have to tear your muscle fibres for them to become stronger.

If you don't go out of your comfort zone, you won't become better at what you do.

It's the only way you'll learn!

So don't give up on making money online – because that rut you're stuck in is challenging you to break through your own barriers.

Break through now and you'll discover a whole new world of success on the other side…

## 9. Think About The Reasons You've Got This Far.

What made you start up your online business?

To never give up on making money online, you have to constantly refuel your motivation.

Your desire to succeed needs to be replenished at every opportunity.

For me, working online just made perfect sense. Here's why I got started:

- You can travel & work wherever you want in the world.

- You're constantly learning and growing.

- You reap the rewards of your hard work.

- It's a character building journey that's helps you become more resilient.

- As a <u>digital nomad</u>, you're surrounded by incredibly inspiring people who want to see you succeed.

- You get to avoid the office politics that comes with a full time job.

- You have far, far more freedom!

- You get to wake up in the morning whenever you want!

…I mean, in what other job do you have the ability to work from home in your underwear whilst making money?

Casual Friday for the
Telecommuter

On a serious note though:

To keep your motivation topped up, you need to understand exactly why you're doing this.

Otherwise you'll give up on making money online because you don't have any drive to achieve the end results.

So think about what motivates you:

…Write down your reasons.

…Keep them in a place where you can see them.

…And never forget the reasons behind why you're living this lifestyle.

10. It Ain't Easy BUT It's Worth It.

If this lifestyle was easy, everyone would be doing it!

But here's the brutal truth:

90% of businesses FAIL.

Not many people make in in business – online or offline. It's a psychological, draining game that most just aren't prepared to deal with.

They want the easy, simple life where they're told when, where and how to work.

But give up on making money online and you'll give up the rewards that come with it.

Because the concept of being successful online is easy.

Putting it into practice is hard.

If you're willing to work hard, you'll make it. You don't even need to spend much time on your online business – you just have to be consistent.

You have to persist – even when the chips are stacked against you.

That's literally the difference between success and failure!

# Chapter 4. 10 Powerful Reasons To Quit Your Job & Start Your Own Business.

Why on earth would you quit your perfectly stable, hard-earned position that pays your bills and keeps your food on the table? Because, thanks to the advancements of the modern age and computer technology, full-time jobs are simply no longer a necessity and more a routine held by the naive and unaware worker bees of today's world that are yet to discover the beauty of passive income.

Working when you want to, how you want to, being the boss of yourself and having total geographical freedom to travel with loved once is the incentive driving many millions of entrepreneurs into ditching their 9-5 for a life of freedom and wealthiness.

This article will explore 10 reasons to quit your job and begin earning online...

## 1. Become the master of your own fate

This is one the best reasons to quit your job right now!

While, yes, full-time jobs may be considered 'secure' and 'stable' ways to earn money, this is a common misconception. Being a worker for your boss is most certainly not a stable way to generate an income.

Regardless of your position, higher up management executives have the power to cast you aside if they see it as being better for their company. Business is a dog-eat-dog world and, if you're considered not to be pulling your weight, managers can easily cut off your 'stable' stream of income and leave you drowning in the deep end.

Don't let this frighten you.

Let it entice you into spreading your roots wider and establishing multiple streams of income. There are a plethora of articles out there ready to educate you in the world of passive income (have a browse around our website and you'll find hundreds of ways to earn online). Read up, learn the facts and escape the slave trade dressed up as 'secure income'.

## 2. Freedom

Simply put, having a business that can be run from any device with internet connection is like being given keys to complete financial freedom.

Having a full-time job will tie you to a nearby location and force you stay there, threatening financial insecurity if you choose to move elsewhere. Abandoning your day job and setting up streams of online income is a great way to have freedom to travel and explore the world, spending your time doing things you actually want to and not working 24/7.

### 3. Quit being a number

It's an unfortunate fact that many workers are treated like numbers – millions of tiny parts that make up a huge whole divided into employers and employees. Even those in high managerial positions are still very much employees with the exception of the CEO. Working for yourself allows you to break this pattern of being another cog in a machine.

### 4. Follow your passion

Countless people spend 70% of their lives in a job they simply don't care about. Society has created a fast-flowing conveyor belt on which people are firmly glued from the age of around four right up until retirement.

Go to school, get an education, get a degree, go to university and work hard to get your grades so that you can get a decent paying job. We've all heard it before and although some have, many don't question the system and follow instructions blindly without considering other options, being told that those that do go on to work independent of a full-time job are the exceptions. This is wrong, and an utter lie.

Break the shackles of society and do it your way – set up your own sources of passive income. Invest some time into getting them started and reap the benefits for a lifetime.

## 5. Technology will replace you

The advancements of our modern technological world pose an unfortunate threat to many human-led careers. Like it or not, computers are replacing many job opportunities and will likely overpower much of our world in the coming years.

Whether it be self-checkout machines, automatically driven taxis or online accounting services, computer technology is advancing at a rapid rate and is encouraging business owners to ditch paying their workers and to invest in technology that does everything for them. Entrepreneurship, however, will not be replaced hence why you should get started with your business as soon as you can.

## 6. Starting a business has never been easier

Really, it hasn't.

There are so, so many different options out there for you to get started online. Dropshipping, retail arbitrage, affiliate marketing, stock investing, selling on Etsy, eBay, Amazon, blogging, writing eBooks – these are, believe it or not, a small handful of the ways in which you can start earning online.

Furthermore, starting a business has never been cheaper! Setting up a profitable, long-lasting business can now be done with as little as a few thousands pounds and, while this may seem steep, you can earn this in very little time with the internet alone.

## 7. Dreams

Have you ever dreamt of having a full-time job that binds you to a city and won't let you leave without sacrificing your annual salary? Of course not.

This is slavery in disguise and we all need to open our eyes to it. Don't let money be your master, take control and start living your dream now.

## 8. You feel like you can't do anything else

Your job is making you feel trapped and like you can never escape. This is a good enough reason as any to quit. You're a human, the most intelligent lifeform known to exist. Don't undermine your capabilities and settle for contentment – be the exception.

## 9. Money is not the key to happiness.

Really, it isn't...And that's one of the most powerful reasons to quit your job & follow your passion.

Countless studies have shown that even the happiness lottery winners fizzles out after a few months or so. You may not become an instant millionaire after quitting your job but you can spend time with your children.

You can go out and spend time doing the things you life. You can go out for meals with your wife and spend your earnings on holidays. Slaving away at a day job for money is not worth it when you have options to do so much more with your time.

## 10. Because you can!

Simple. You can achieve your dream, so why wouldn't you?

# Chapter 5. 10 Easy Ways To Make Money Online.

With all information known to man at our fingertips and portable devices that allow us to tap into the web almost anywhere, there are a tonne of ways you can earn money online with very little effort.

This article teach you 10 easy ways to make money online...

10 Easy Ways To Make Money Online:

1. **Matched Betting**. Don't panic – I'm not suggesting you blow all of your money on gambling in the hope of earning big. Believe it or not, this is a top pick for easy ways to make money online! Tonnes of betting agencies offer free bets when you bet using them (bet £20 and receive a free £20 bet, for example. By taking advantage of these free bets you can earn serious amounts of money for doing virtually nothing. Coral.co.uk are offering £20 worth of free bets for betting just £5 which is just one of a tonne of free-bet offers out there. Search around and make the most of these while you still can!

2. **Surveys**. A classic way of earning money online is through surveys. They require incredibly little effort and can be done from literally anywhere with wi-fi. The great

thing about using online surveys is that you can do as many as you wish and whenever you wish. You're not tied into doing a set amount per day/week and can simply just log in, power through a couple and get paid whenever you have a few moments to spare. Opinion Outpost and SurveyMonkey are the most reputable platforms for surveying. Just set up and account, put in your details and get going free of charge!

3. **Blogging**. Blogging is an excellent way not only to earn money online but to promote other business/products you already sell. A blog is simply just a website to which you post regular content, or 'blog posts', to your audience. You may decide to run a travel blog and post about where to go on holiday, perhaps you run a blog all about football and updates for your favourite teams – whatever it is make sure you choose a specialised niche to maximise your traffic. WordPress and Squarespace offer low prices for excellent website-creation tools to help you get started.

4. **Rewards cards.** Rewards cards are a super simple way of earning money for making no changes to your daily routine and simply doing exactly what you already do anyway. Rewards cards will award you points every time you spend money (Costa offer a card that gives you 10 points every time you spend £1, for example) that can

be redeemed on a whole host of prizes – free hotel rooms, holidays, gift cards – the list is endless. Rewards cards such as the Sapphire Preferred Card will give you a free $500 if you spend $4,000 within 90 days. If you're likely to spend this much anyway then you're essentially getting given free money!

5. **Selling**. Having a search around your attic (and wherever else you put unused items) to find items that could be sold is a super easy way to make money and free up some space in your house. Reselling old phones, clothes, whatever it is you can find will earn you a surprisingly high amount of cash. Sites such as Ebay and Gumtree are your best bet for reselling and offer fairly low listing fees too, maximising your profits and earning you more cash.

6. **Advertising**. Advertising can be done in a variety of forms – affiliate marketing, AdSense and direct-selling. Tonnes of companies offer affiliate market programs that you can sign up to simply by having a website. They'll email you affiliate links to put onto your site and, when people click on your site, you'll be paid commissions for the money earned by the company. AdSense is a scheme run by Google that allows you to choose ads that relate to your niche and, again, receive commission for each click made.

7. **Upwork & Fiverr.** Upwork and Fiverr are sites that allow employers to publish ads for jobs they have available. If you're skilled in writing, programming, website creation – practically anything then there's guaranteed to be a job opportunity out there for you. I've completed a tonne of jobs through Upwork – all of which have been done entirely through my laptop. If you love the thought of freelancing and working in your pyjamas/in coffee shops, these websites are definitely for you.

8. **Create a course.** Using a website such as Udemy you can create your very own course to sell at a price. If you're particularly knowledgeable in a certain area then you most certainly can turn your knowledge into an unlimited source of passive income. Simply converting what you already know into a comprehensive guide hugely increase your monthly profits. Udemy even have a free course on how to create your first course!

9. **Ebooks.** Are you looking for easy ways to make money online passively? Writing an ebook can take as little as a few weeks and can earn you money for as long as you live. Simply browsing Amazon's Kindle store to see which books are selling most frequently at the moment and creating a book to match this demand is a super easy and relatively time-efficient way of earning. Check out our guide on how to write an ebook to get started!

10. **Website flipping**. Buying domain names, improving them and selling them at an increased price is another great way to earn some extra cash. It's one of the most popular picks for easy ways to make money online. Simply browse around for sites that are for sale that may have some potential for adding value, drop in some affiliate links & AdSense campaigns, earn as much as you can from the site and sell it when it begins to run dry. It's really that simple.

# Chapter 6. How To Get Rich From Nothing.

We all want to earn more money. Whether it's to fund holidays, buy a new car, pay off a mortgage – increasing your annual income is a great way to relieve stress and do more with your time.

Unfortunately, many of us shy away from great opportunities to earn because we're scared to fail. Making investments into companies that could lose value and devoting time to writing a book that might not work out seems like an incredibly daunting task and one that few of us choose to go through with. However, living an entirely risk-free life is exactly what leaves many of us dissatisfied and unhappy with our current position.

Thankfully, not all methods of earning are incredibly risky and many are a lot easier than most of us think. You no longer have to be a stock-exchange expert or be born into royalty to become a millionaire.

This article will run you through some excellent, fool-proof ways that will teach you how to get rich from nothing…

Goals

Before you embark on any journey you need to decide where you're going. It's no good just grabbing all the money from wherever you can if you're hoping to make some serious long-term cash.

First things first, you need to establish your goals. Where do you want to be in a year's time?

Perhaps you hope to double your monthly income before you hit your next age milestone. Maybe you want to have put away your first million by the time you're 65. Whatever your goal is, you need to stay committed to it.

Keep track of your monthly expenses and earnings and try to always keep a sensible gap between them. Save with the intention of being able to get by for the next couple of years if all of your current sources of income are cut off. If you spend £3,000 a month, try to keep at least £24,000 saved up in the bank.

This way, even if you do suffer some serious losses on your journey you'll always have some cash to fall back on.

How To Get Rich From Nothing: Investing
First and foremost, investing your savings is a sure way to allow you to build up your savings overtime.

You should aim to put away at least 10% of your monthly earnings into savings. Make sure you do not touch these savings – don't dip into them if you need a holiday or a new car or whatever it may be. These are your investment funds.

Take these funds and invest them into companies. Buying shares in companies will prevent your cash from gathering dust and will allow you to earn passively without having to actually do anything.

Investing through your bank or putting savings into a Roth IRA is a great way to generate passive income and will free up your time so that you can diversify your efforts and establish multiple streams of revenue.

Above investing in companies, you should always remember to invest in yourself. Spend the money you do have on improving your skills, learning about finances and increasing your worth as an individual, not just an entrepreneur.

How To Get Rich From Nothing: Make Use of Your Talents

Even if they haven't yet discovered it yet, everybody is talented in one area or another. The area which you feel most passionate about is typically that which you're most knowledgeable in, therefore utilising your talents to earn you money is an excellent place to begin.

Perhaps you're particularly skilled in writing or playing a musical instrument. Using this talent as a launchpad for your financial journey will not only give you some valuable tools to begin with but will also ensure that the area of expertise you're pursuing is one that you actually care about.

How To Get Rich From Nothing: Establish Multiple Streams of Revenue

Many, many people make the mistake of relying solely on a single source of income. However, if ever this stream were to be cut off then most of us would have nothing to fall back on.

The entrepreneurs key to success is never to put all of their eggs in one basket – rather splitting their 'eggs', so to speak, amongst multiple baskets. Perhaps you already have a well paid position at your current workplace that earns you enough to get by. Rather than depending entirely on this single position to supply all of your financial needs, spread your earnings across a variety of independent sources.

This can be done in a variety of ways that don't have to involve increasing your weekly hours at another day job. Maybe you choose to set up an online business in the form of a blog, website or store. All three of these sources will earn you passive income that does not require you to actually 'go into' work every day. Once set up, these sources of income will provide a steady stream of income on their own.

Of course, building up multiple streams of income will take time to complete at first and you will be putting in a significant number of hours to begin with. However, once up and running these methods will supply you with constant cash for no more work at all – earning you far more than you would normally receive from a day job.

And there you have it – a handful of super easy tips to help you diversify your income and begin your journey towards getting rich in the next year. As always, stay consistent with your efforts and don't shy away from earning in the face of defeat. You may well suffer losses however just remember these are all part of your journey to financial freedom.

# Chapter 7. Money Affirmations.

Many people have sufficient knowledge of how to make money yet they simply don't. There are a tonne of articles out there revolving around earning money, establishing multiple streams of revenue, stocks and trades, you name it, however people **still** settle for the norm. A 9-5, earned income lifestyle that ties its workers to one location and threatens them with financial turmoil if they dare to leave. So, if there exist ways to escape this norm, many of which you have likely already heard of before considering you've reached this article, *what on earth is holding everybody back?*

The answer – attitude. Success originates in the mind and lacking in the correct attitude is a guaranteed way to limit your financial growth. This article will explain exactly how you can adjust your perspective to attract wealth in all areas and persevere when streams run drier than usual.

Money Affirmations: The Importance of Your Brain...
Positive affirmations are simple, short statements that, when read repeatedly, help to reprogram your subconscious mind to integrate a particular belief. Your brain is a lot like a maze of winding paths. The more a walkway is utilized, the more downtrodden the grass that covers it will become and thus the more that path will be automatically used. Let me rephrase that a little more clearly – if walking in the woods, you are far more likely to follow pathways that have been used frequently rather than taking disused, overgrown routes. Your brain is a sea of intertwining pathways that work in this exact manner.

Every single brain is filled with trillions (yes, *trillions)* of tiny cells called 'neurons'. These neurons, when activated, send electrical signals that, in turn, cause some sort of change in your body. Your brain builds clusters of these neurons over time so that it can operate more efficiently. If you saw a dog, for example, you would not need to recall all of your past experiences with four legged creatures, identify its ears and snout and wait for it to bark to conclude that, yes, this animal is a dog. No, your brain instantly recognises this animal as a dog because it has a section of neurons dedicated to this knowledge. Clever.

Now, here's the key bit. These neuronal pathways act as great shortcuts to make things run more smoothly upstairs. However, the brain is, of course, a finite space that cannot house endless amounts of neurons. Therefore, when a pathway is not used, it is lost. Alternatively, and most importantly, if a pathway is used frequently then it becomes stronger. **Your brain will automatically use that pathway without you consciously having to choose to do so.**

**...And Why This is Relevant**

Now you may be wondering what on earth this information has to do with wealth and earning money. Brains are naturally negative, pessimistic machines and are built this way to ensure our survival (more on this another time). Therefore, naturally, if you suffer from a financial loss, you will naturally wish to pull out of a project to prevent any further losses. Strengthening your neural pathways is absolutely key to building a positive attitude towards your financial journeys and, in turn, increasing your wealth. Positive affirmations are the perfect way to change your brain's natural assumptions and to switch your vision to focus on the positive rather than the negative. This process abandons pessimistic neural pathways and builds fresh, positive shortcuts for your brain to take. Through practice, you will no longer automatically think pessimistically and will begin to see things differently.

How to Use Money Affirmations
So what exactly *is* a positive <u>affirmation</u>?

An affirmation is a short, positive statement that you make to yourself frequently to rewire your subconscious brain. Examples may include, 'I am in control of my happiness' or 'I am wealthy'. It's best to formulate your own affirmations that are specific to your beliefs and goals. Focus on what you hope for and would like to achieve and base your affirmations on this. I would recommend aiming to have a list of around 3-5 affirmations tailored to your goals.

After building a bank of affirmations, write them down somewhere easily accessible – perhaps in a notebook or on your phone. You should aim to read through these affirmations around 2-3 times for 3 minutes, every single day for the next couple of months. I recommend reading them just before bed and right after waking up as your subconscious mind is most active during these times.

Examples Of Money Affirmations
Although it's best to think of your own affirmations that suit you, below are a list of popular ones that you may choose if you wish.

- Money is good, I love money
- I am consciously happy and positive about money.
- Money is simply an energy that allows me freedom
- I attract money naturally to me. I am a money magnet
- I am not a slave to money. Money is attracted to me.
- I am wealthy and abundant.

# Chapter 8. How To Attract Wealth - The Law Of Attraction.

The focal point for those who have already had success in the <u>Law of Attraction</u> or those who are first timers looking to unravel more information about the Laws of Attraction are most likely "Money" and "Wealth."

Today's society has taught us from childhood, that the goal in life or "American Dream" is to be the richest by unlawful means or "Life or Death" sacrifices. Were you a child that often watched your parents struggle financially? Watching your parents live life payday to payday can be tough yet, effective on your adulthood.

Most parents often feel that they will never get out of debt, or be financially stable, so they teach that lifestyle to they're kids. It makes perfect sense!

Although, those going down a great path in life are dreaming for things such as: great health, great passion for their jobs or careers, Happy marriages, and let's not forget financial freedom. When your life is in order financially, you really get to think about what's important in life! Not only do you get to think about what you want out of life, but you can also live stress free and burden free. One thing to always keep in mind if you want wealth is to be a positive thinker and bring a "Take charge" attitude! Procrastinating never got anybody, anywhere. Having a positive attitude is often the backbone to The Law of Attraction.

How To Attract Wealth: The Law Of Attraction

Author, <u>Wallace D. Wattles</u>, was one of the first to show a outstanding impact that The Law of Attraction can have on any financial situation. Wallace published a book called " The Science of Getting Rich" in 1910. In Wallace's book, he discussed how mental stability can effect financial wealth.

Other great author's who have shown or proven that The Law of Attraction can have a tremendous impact on all financial situations are <u>Prentice Mulford</u>. He was an author and humorist. He had a collage of essays on The Law of Attraction. These essays were called "Some Laws of Health and Beauty", "Good", and lastly "Ill Effects of Thought." These were all written in 1891. <u>Ralph Waldo Trine</u> was an American author, lecturer and salesman. Ralph was also good friends with Henry Ford; they both enjoyed the discussion of success. Ralph published his book " In Tune with the Infinite " in 1897. Lastly, <u>Thomas Troward</u> was in my opinion, the most strongest influence and had the hardest impact on The New Thoughts Movement. He was English author who wrote an published 6 books in his lifetime. Although, the book that refers to the topic of The Law of Attraction is "The Law and the World" published in 1917.

One thing to know is that it's fairly hard to follow The Laws of Attraction without it going unnoticed. People fail to realize that wealth isn't just about the money! Wealth can be gained in numerous ways such as: hard work, education, appearance and the list goes on. The key goal is to aim for peace, and positivity in your love life, health, and career. After you've got your personal life in order, you will be a magnet to financial success!

How To Attract Wealth: Don't Be A Victim!

Stop blaming everyone for your financial problems. The lifestyle you're currently living was not chosen for you. You have or had the same opportunity as the next rich guy, so start making plans and goals for yourself to accomplish. And let's actually accomplish them with no excuses or hesitations. Let your mind become overcrowded with thoughts of money. Get ecstatic when you come in contact with any bills and be grateful for the ones you have!

How To Attract Wealth: Create More Abundance!
If you have a hard time getting in the money spirit, here are a few things you may be willing to try. Write abundance checks to yourself.

Once a month fill out a check with your name and a amount of your preference, etc. Then sign it under whatever name you wish! Not a real name, a silly name like "Fairly Godmother."

Next, try not to constantly get the needy feeling for money...

...Feeling needy will only create more financial problems for you in the long run. Next on the list is to be in a joyful or happy mood. Don't you often realize when you're happy, you become a magnet to great things? It's like you become lucky.

Then, change your pessimistic mindset to a positive one. When you say I "can't" afford it, you're really just worsening your chances for becoming able to afford it later. So start telling to yourself I "can" afford it! Lastly, For now on, when you see money lying around, grab it! That money was put in mid- air just for you. Or pretend the money found you! "Grab it, It's yours!"

How To Attract Wealth: Let It Flow To You
Money can be compared to a lot of things but I've never heard of it being compared to electricity! Although, money has it as ways of being just like electricity.

Many people blame money for their mistakes and are afraid to face their everyday responsibilities. Everything you want to manifest requires spirituality accordingly. Spirituality is an intense feeling as well as a healthy and balanced love for something, especially money. Keep pictures or symbols of money in your mind to keep you focused and to help remind yourself of why you even started what you did! Always remember, before you take action, think it through.

Your subconsiousness is to be put to the test when leading you to the right path of actions. Lastly imagine you would feel like if you were wealthy. Think about real numbers and commas, make it the main thought in your mind of how rich you want to be. If you have these thoughts regularly, do it at a time that works best with your schedule!

# Chapter 9. Why You Don't Need Money to Make Money.

**Here's the truth – you don't need money to make money!**

Many, many people are reluctant to create a business (or even *think* about creating a business) for fear of high investment costs. It's a common myth that starting a business requires money, however this just simply is not the case. This article will show you just how easy it is to start your very own entrepreneurial empire without having to sell a kidney to fund it.

**Why You Don't Need Money To Make Money: Tools For Creating a Business**

- The right mindset. The key to any success is persistence and perseverance. You **must** be willing to invest your time if not your money – although businesses may generate their own passive income over time, you will need to put a fair amount of elbow grease to begin with. Hard work always pays off.
- Thinking in the long term. Thinking in years rather than days will massively boost your motivation and drive to keep going with your business. Although entrepreneurialism isn't a get-rich-quick scheme, it will, with time and effort, give you total freedom to travel the world and make the most of your time will still generating a full-time income.
- Supply and demand. Is your niche taking advantage of something which people will want and will pay for, or is it based solely on your personal interests rather than those of others? It is important to match the needs of the market and to fill a hole in the industry that is not currently being filled.
- Don't make excuses! Your excuses are your personal barriers – claiming that your business will not work because you have

'no time', 'no money', 'no good ideas' is a defeatist attitude that will only set you up for failure. Your beliefs about what will happen will massively influence the reality you create for yourself. For example, if you believe that you will 'never create a successful business' you will limit yourself with this mindset. If you truly do not believe you are able to create a successful business, you will likely put in far less effort into making this wish a reality and thus *will never create a successful business*. Believe in yourself. You are more than capable of achieving your dreams – your future self has already achieved them and is waiting for you to make the right decisions. Make them.

**Your Dream**

Your future is your control – you seriously don't need money to make money. That is a fact. Everybody has a dream, somewhere, even if you haven't uncovered it yet. That dream is your destiny, it is what you were put here to accomplish.

**Do not let the limiting that "you need money to make money" hold you back**.

You may need to start small to work your way up. Maybe you wish to start a new healthy fast food business, entirely vegan friendly. As we said before, you need to focus on years rather than days. Start small, maybe start through making vegan snacks to sell to your local community, or drafting an eBook about how to cook your favourite meals as a vegan. Work your way up from here – as you climb higher you will be able to achieve more and money will come, it really will. The key, though, is not to do it for the money, do it for the dream. Do it for yourself.

**Starting A Business Without Money**

While mindset and mentality is absolutely key to creating a successful business without money, you're probably wondering how exactly do you go about doing so.

Below are a number of different starting points for you to begin with.

**1. Creating**

If you have any level of skill in arts and crafts, creating things to sell can be a great place to start. Although gathering materials in order to create may involve some costs, these products can then be sold for far more than they cost to make. Many huge companies started out through simply making things to sell.

The best places online to sell your products easily are Etsy, Abe's Market, Bonanza and eBay. These sites can also be a great place to search for ideas and inspiration.

**2. Reselling**

If you're not the artsy type and don't have space to store products, reselling can be a great way to earn money as a retailer rather than a manufacturer.

Dropshipping is a great way to earn money through resales. Dropshipping is the process of advertising a product that you do not own. When this product is purchased, you place an order from a wholesaler and have the product shipped directly to the customer. This way, you never actually handle the product but still make a profit through selling it at a higher price than it is purchased at.

Browsing thrift stores and antique shops can also be a great way to find products to resell at a higher price. Oftentimes, shops of this nature stock items that they know little about and thus do not sell them as highly as they could. You, a reseller, can take full advantage of this.

## 3. Maximising your expertise

Another great way to earn money is to sell your services. If you are skilled in a particular area, say, mechanics or playing a musical instrument (or speaking English, French, writing poetry – anything you can do well) then you could sell these skills to other people. This way, you can earn through teaching somebody to do something you love doing anyway. Selling your services requires no startup costs and could lead to developing a successful business further down the line. Even if a business is not started, this can be a great way to earn some cash to help you start your business.

It's clear to see that the belief that "you need money to make money" is a common misconception. There are a wealth of methods to not only starting your business but earning money to fund it without having to put any in. Take each of these methods and make them your own. Find what works best for you and the money will come.

# Chapter 10. Wealth Consciousness.

Wealth consciousness is an incredibly powerful tool for increasing your riches...

...Consciousness in itself is an awareness of something. If you are conscious, you are aware of your surroundings; if you are self-conscious, you are aware of yourself and likely focussing your attention on your image. If you are *wealth* conscious, you are aware of your wealth.

People that are wealth conscious are not so just because they are wealthy. Being conscious of your wealth does not require any sum of money, moreover it determines how a person will regard their financial losses and gains. A person that is wealth conscious likely will not go extended periods having very little money as they are aware of their income and outcome and will manage their spending. Wealth consciousness is a mindset that acts as a magnet, a way of thinking that will ensure a person remains financially stable at all times.

Being conscious and being mindful are often considered the same thing, and this assumption is fair. Mindfulness is a state of being that ignores the past and the future and focuses on the here and now. In reality, the present is the only moment that truly exists because both the past and and the future are fleeting and yet to be experienced.

Wealth Consciousness & Meditation
Meditation is the practice of bringing the attention to the present moment and is key to becoming wealth conscious for it enables us to live fully in the here and now. There are a whole load of meditation practices around, some focusing on the breath as a tool to direct the attention to the present, others using physical movements such as

yoga. Find which practice suits you and dedicate a small (or large, depending on your availability) time slot each day to it – whether it be twenty minutes, ten, five ( there are even *one* minute meditation methods out there!) – every little really does help.

To give you a brief overview of the practice of meditation, I will outline a method I use and have found to be successful in reducing anxiety and boosting mindfulness.

1. Find a comfortable, seated position in which you will not be disturbed.
2. Close your eyes and take deep breaths, breathing into your stomach/abdomen rather than the chest.
3. With every in-breath, count one, and two with every out-breath. Focus your attention entirely on your breath, feeling the sensations over your body as the breath enters and exists. You may find it easiest to focus on the tingles around the nostrils as the breath moves through them, or to focus on the inflation of the stomach with every inhale. Whatever works for you – there is not right or wrong method.
4. Try to dismiss any thoughts that come to mind. There will be many, this is okay. Try not to judge your thoughts, marking them as unhelpful or bad, or even positive. Just allow them to float freely over you and recognise them as being separate from you – you are not your thoughts.
5. Continue this practice for as long as you wish. There is no time limit. I try to meditate for at least ten minutes a day and find that to be just right. Find what works for you.
6. Repeat. Repetition is key and if you do not intend to meditate daily then I wouldn't recommend meditating at all. Thoughts may fly straight away, 'I don't have time for this', 'I have so much work to do and I'm sat here thinking about breathing'. **These are just thoughts, they are not you**. Think of yourself as a mountain. Clouds may pass over you, but they are not you. Your thoughts are the clouds.

How To Boost Your Wealth Consciousness
1. An important step to take is to quit avoiding money, brushing it under the carpet and acting as though your payments are being made from some invisible source that replenishes itself. Look your money in it's eyes for what it is. You are not bound by your income, it does not control you and you should not fear it – just be conscious of it. Keep a track of your earnings and losses and don't be afraid to check your bank balance. I would recommend opening a spreadsheet (I use Google Sheets) to keep a loose track of your financial developments. In doing this, you can increase your income steadily simply by controlling and being aware of your transactions.
2. Have a conversation with your future, financially stable self. How have they got to this place? What attitudes have they had towards money to get there? Create that reality.
3. Do not feel guilty about making money. The premise that a rich man cannot enter the gates of heaven is simply a myth. While yes, giving to charities and spending on others is essential – it is essential for personal growth and happiness and keeping balance in the world, you should not feel guilty for earning money and saving money. There are many ways of giving, spending money is certainly a less significant way than, say, giving love and support to others. If you wish to be charitable then give gifts richer than wealth and do not feel guilty for earning money.
4. Wealth that has not been earned will not stay. If money was simply given to you, let's say you won a million on the lottery, you would not have developed the intelligence to keep hold of it. The process of earning money through putting in effort develops your values for it and, in turn, your ability to sustain it. Hard work is important in any field, including earning money. There is a difference, though, between hard work and worthwhile work. While you may slave 56 weekly hours at a full-time job, you are not maximising your earning potential. Work of this nature does not encourage personal growth.

Working smart, however, will initiate a positive multiplier effect that will increase your profit overtime.

For more on working smart through establishing multiple revenue streams, **click here**.